PUBLIC LIBRARY DISTRICT OF COLUMBIA

Living Religions

Sikhism

Jon Mayled

© Copyright 2003 Raintree
Published by Raintree, a division of Reed Elsevier, Inc.

All rights reserved. No part of this book may be reproduced or utilized in any form or by any means, electronic or mechanical, including photocopying, recording, or by any information storage and retrieval system, without permission in writing from the Publishers. Inquiries should be addressed to:

Raintree, 100 N. LaSalle St., Suite 1200, Chicago, IL 60602

Library of Congress Cataloging-in-Publication Data:

Mayled, Jon. *6077   0211*
  Sikhism / Jon Mayled.
      v. cm. -- (Living religions)
Includes bibliographical references and index.
Contents: An introduction to Sikhism -- Guru Nanak Dev Ji 1 -- Guru Nanak Dev Ji 2 -- The Gurus 1 -- The Gurus 2 -- Guru Gobind Singh Ji -- Sikh leaders -- Sikh beliefs about God -- Sikh beliefs about life -- Signs and symbols 1 -- Signs and symbols 2 -- The Gurdwara -- The Langar -- Worship 1 -- Worship 2 -- The Guru Granth Sahib Ji -- Festivals 1 -- Festivals 2 -- Pilgrimage 1 -- Pilgrimage 2 -- Growing Up -- Marriage -- Death -- Creation -- Environment -- Human Rights -- Service to Others 1-Sewa -- Service to Others 2 -- Women in Sikhism.
  ISBN 0-7398-6387-8 (Library Binding-Hardcover)
  1. Sikhism--Juvenile literature. [1. Sikhism.] I. Title. II. Series.
  BL2018 .M56 2003
  294.6--dc21
                            2002152099

Printed and bound in China.

07 06 05 04 03
10 9 8 7 6 5 4 3 2 1

Acknowledgments:

The publishers would like to thank the following for permission to use photographs:

The Environmental Picture Library/Graham Burns, p. 50; TRIP/H. Luther, pp. 45, 56; TRIP/Resource Foto, p. 48; TRIP/H. Rogers, pp. 2, 5, 6, 7, 8, 9, 10 (right), 12, 13, 19,
20 (both), 21, 23, 24, 25, 28, 29, 49, 52, 54, 55, 58, 59; Harjinder Singh Sagoo, pp. 3, 10 (left), 14, 15, 18, 26, 27, 30, 31, 32, 33, 34, 35, 36, 37, 38, 40, 41, 42, 43, 44, 46, 47, 53, 57; TRIP/R. Westlake, p. 51.

The publishers have made every effort to contact copyright holders. However, if any material has been incorrectly acknowledged, the publishers would be pleased to correct this at the earliest opportunity.

Contents

An Introduction to Sikhism

In this section you will:

- learn about and understand what faith and trust mean to Sikhs;
- consider the ways in which Sikhism seeks to strengthen faith in Waheguru (God);
- think about the topic of truth and religion.

Faith and trust

The people who follow Sikhism are called **Sikhs.** The word "Sikh" means a disciple, someone who tries to follow the teachings of a particular leader. In the case of Sikhism, these are the teachings of the **Gurus.**

All Sikhs have faith and trust in God, called **Waheguru**—"Wonderful Lord," the God who created all things.

Like all other religions, Sikhism is based on a system of beliefs. Beliefs are things that people think to be true, even if there is little evidence to support the beliefs.

Believing in something means that a person has faith and trust in what they believe. Faith is a firm and honest belief that goes beyond all else. Trust is the certainty that what a person believes is right, a complete confidence in something, or a certainty that we will not be let down, as when we trust our best friends.

A way of life

Sikhs believe that their religion is a way of life. They believe that God created all things, and that God provided guidance to help all people live good lives according to the beliefs of Sikhism. So, to be a true Sikh means to accept God and to carry out God's will.

Sikhism teaches that all people are equal in the eyes of God and each other. One of the main aims of Sikhism is that there should be a united human society living together in peace and equality and following the teachings of God. In particular, Sikhs believe in **sewa**—selfless service for others.

Sikhism intends to give freedom of thought to all believers. It aims to free people from the round of rebirth by helping them to reach **mukti,** or spiritual freedom in their lives. They do this by responding to God with love and obedience.

Poster showing the ten Gurus

Like other religions, Sikhism also aims to free the human self from vanity and greed, from envy and tension, from fear and insecurity. Through following the teachings of God, Sikhism seeks to free people from the worship of false gods and low desires, and shows them the hope of goodness and excellence leading to spiritual liberation, or freedom. Sikhs are certain of their faith because they believe that Waheguru has been revealed through the teachings of the Gurus.

The first of these Gurus was **Guru Nanak Dev Ji,** To show respect to the Gurus, Sikhs add the words Ji or Dev Ji, meaning "Honored Sir" to the names of the Gurus. The word "Guru" has two syllables—the first, "gu," means darkness, and the second, "ru," means light. A Guru is, therefore, someone who helps others in their transition from darkness to light.

Sikh women in the gurdwara

Truth and religion

Faith, belief, and trust are essential to all religions. Religions depend on truth, but there are different types of truth. Scientific truth is the easiest: When an experiment can be repeated over and over again with the same results, this establishes a truth. Historical truth is when there is evidence to prove that a particular event took place in the past. Moral truth depends on the idea that people instinctively "know" what is right or wrong. Artistic truth is found in novels, pictures, and films, when a work of fiction appears to be true to the way in which humans behave. Finally, there is religious truth. People who believe in a religion follow its teachings so that they can discover their own truth about God.

If we knew that the teachings of a religion were true, we would not just have to believe in a god because we would know, as a fact, that this god existed. Although religious people may say that they "know" that their god exists, this is based on faith and belief, not on fact. It is this belief that, with faith and trust in a god, makes the whole idea of religion different from any other sort of belief people may have.

Guru Nanak Dev Ji 1

Map of northwest India showing the modern-day state of Punjab

In this section you will:

- begin to learn about the Sikh Gurus;
- find out about the early life of Guru Nanak Dev Ji;
- start to understand the teachings that he gave to his followers.

There are six major religions in the world: Buddhism, Christianity, Hinduism, Islam, Judaism, and Sikhism. Sikhism, the youngest of these religions, was founded by **Guru Nanak Dev Ji** in the fifteenth century.

The **Sikh** faith came about through the teachings of the ten Sikh **Gurus.** They are all respected by Sikhs, but they are not worshiped because they were human beings, not gods. Sikhs also recognize that, in addition to the Gurus, there have been other messengers from God, such as the Buddha, Jesus, and Muhammad (pbuh).

Sikhs believe that the Gurus were all very special people who did not need to be reborn in the cycle of reincarnation, but were sent back to earth to become God's messengers.

All the Gurus taught that there is only one God, that all people are equally important before God, and that everyone can attain **mukti** (spiritual liberation) through living their lives with love and being faithful and obedient to God.

Guru Nanak Dev Ji's childhood

Guru Nanak Dev Ji was born in 1469 at Talwandi in the Punjab, India. Talwandi was later renamed Nankana Sahib in his honor and is now in the state of Pakistan.

When Nanak was born, astrologers said that he would grow up to be someone very special who would lead other people toward God. Nanak's father, Mehta Kalu, was a Hindu and so he brought up his son to follow that religion. However, from an early age, Nanak rejected the many rituals and customs that are part of Hinduism and other religions.

When Nanak was five years old, he was sent to school. Tradition tells that his teacher, Gopal Das, wrote the letters of the alphabet on a slate and Nanak asked what each letter meant. The teacher said that the letters themselves did not mean anything, and he asked Nanak what he

thought the letters meant. Nanak went through the alphabet and used each letter as the start of a verse of poetry in praise of God. This hymn can be read today in the Sikh scriptures, the **Guru Granth Sahib Ji.** The teacher was amazed at his pupil's understanding of God and his command of language. He realized at once that Nanak was no ordinary child.

When a Hindu boy reaches the age of about eleven he is given a sacred thread to wear. Nanak refused to wear it, saying that a thread could break, and that what he wanted was "the sacred thread that after the death of a man accompanies his soul to the next world."

He went on to say: "Make kindness the material, and spin the thread of contentment. Tie knots of truth and virtue. These qualities in a person are the real sacred thread."

On one occasion, Nanak's father sent him to a nearby town and gave him some money, which he was told to spend wisely. On the way Nanak met some holy men. He asked them how they could live without food, homes, or jobs. The men told him that they had no need of these things because God provided for them. Nanak thought about this and, when he arrived at the town, he spent his money on food for the men.

When Nanak returned home, his father was angry because he had intended that his son should invest the money, not give it away.

An ordinary human

It is important to remember that Sikhs show great honor and respect towards the person of Guru Nanak Dev Ji and that, with the other Gurus, he is given the title Dev Ji. However, it is equally important to remember that, although he was the founder of Sikhism, he was an ordinary human being. Sikhs do not believe that Guru Nanak Dev Ji was a god, and this idea would be very insulting to them. Guru Nanak Dev Ji was a great leader, as was Muhammad in Islam. He showed his followers the way to reach God, but it must never be suggested that he was a god himself. The earliest details we have about Guru Nanak Dev Ji come from Janam-Sakhis, or "life stories," which were written 50 to 80 years after his death.

We know that Nanak was born in 1469 C.E. His father was a tax collector and a Hindu belonging to the Kshatriya caste. Nanak's education was in Hinduism and Islam.

It is also important to remember that Guru Nanak Dev Ji was born a Hindu and that it was his desire to bring together Hindus and Muslims that led to his seeking a new religion.

Guru Nanak Dev Ji, the first Guru

Guru Nanak Dev Ji 2

In this section you will:

- develop an understanding of the importance of Guru Nanak Dev Ji's life and work;
- consider the ways in which Sikhism stresses equality;
- read about Guru Nanak Dev Ji's journeys.

One of the most important events in the life of **Guru Nanak Dev Ji** happened when he was 30 years old. Early every morning, Nanak went to the river to bathe and to pray. One day he did not return at his usual time. His friends went to the river and found his clothes on the bank, but there was no sign of Nanak. Three days later, he reappeared at the same place, but said nothing of what had happened to him during this period.

After this event, Guru Nanak Dev Ji left his home and family, and traveled around the country teaching and preaching. He said that the way he lived was the way that God wanted. He traveled for twenty years, visiting Hindu and Muslim holy places on his journeys.

Guru Nanak Dev Ji taught that everyone should worship the same God, and that every person was equal and should be treated equally. He said there was "no Hindu and no Muslim because everyone was equal in God's eyes."

He also said that those who followed him should always be prepared to work hard to serve God. He taught that human life is our chance to meet the creator through having absolute love and devotion to God.

Guru Nanak Dev Ji also taught that arrogance, pride, lust, anger, greed, and concerns about possessions all take us away from God. He tried to show people that rituals, idol worship, prejudice about people's **caste** (the belief that people are born into different social groups), and any type of oppression was wrong and would prevent people from reaching God.

Guru Nanak Dev Ji visited many Hindu holy places on his travels, including Varanasi in India

Guru Angad Dev Ji, the second Guru

In 1520 Guru Nanak Dev Ji went to live in the village of Kartarpur in the Punjab. Here he set up the first Sikh community.

A man called Bhai Lehna was making a pilgrimage to a Hindu shrine when he met Guru Nanak Dev Ji. He was impressed by Guru Nanak Dev Ji's teachings and became one of his closest followers.

Lehna decided to visit Guru Nanak Dev Ji at Kartarpur. He was wearing his best clothes as he approached the village. The people were gathering grass in the fields, and there was one very muddy bundle left. Lehna picked up the bundle and carried it to the village. Guru Nanak Dev Ji's wife was horrified to see the visitor carrying the muddy bundle, but Guru Nanak Dev Ji told her that it was not a bundle of grass but "a crown to honor the best of men." After this, Lehna never left Guru Nanak Dev Ji, becoming his follower, or disciple.

When Guru Nanak Dev Ji realized that he was about to die, he decided to test the faith of each of his followers to choose someone who could continue his work. He picked Lehna, choosing him even above his own two sons.

He called together **Sikhs** from across the country and blessed Lehna, giving him the name Angad, which means "part of me." He then announced that, from that day, Bhai Lehna would be known as Guru Angad Dev Ji, the second Guru.

Teachings and travel

Apart from the Janam-Sakhis (life stories), there are very few details of Guru Nanak Dev Ji's life. These stories say that, after leaving school, Nanak worked as an accountant for an Afghan chieftain at Sultanpur. He composed hymns while he was there, and a Muslim servant called Mardana, who played the rebab (a stringed instrument with a bow), set them to music.

It was while he was in Sultanpur that Nanak, with Mardana, set up a kitchen where everyone could eat, whether Muslim or Hindu. This was the beginning of the idea of the **langar.**

Sikh tradition says that Nanak went on four long journeys during his life. He traveled east to Assam, south to Ceylon (Sri Lanka); north to Ladakh and Tibet; and west to Mecca, al-Medinah, and Baghdad.

Guru Nanak Dev Ji's teachings said that everyone was equal, and that everyone should be prepared to work hard in order to serve God. He said that human life gave people the only chance to prove themselves worthy to meet God—**Waheguru**—and so to achieve **mukti.** Although Guru Nanak Dev Ji believed in reincarnation and the constant cycle of life and death, he rejected much of Hinduism. In particular, he thought that the Hindu caste system was a form of oppression and was therefore against the will of God.

The Gurus 1

In this section you will:

- learn about the lives of some of the other Sikh Gurus, and how they developed Sikhism;
- learn about the teachings of these Gurus.

Guru Angad Dev Ji (1539–1352)

Guru Angad Dev Ji collected all the hymns of **Guru Nanak Dev Ji** and wrote them down, along with some of his own, in the **Gurmukhi** script. Gurmukhi is the name given to the script in which the Punjabi language is written.

Guru Angad Dev Ji encouraged **Sikhs** to take part in sport regularly, believing that a healthy body and a healthy mind were both important to God.

Guru Amar Das Ji (1552–1574)

Bhai Amar Das was 60 years old when he met Guru Angad Dev Ji. He was a devout Hindu, but the truth of the teachings in the Guru's **shabads** (hymns) made him realize that he could serve his God only through true devotion and love, and so he changed his whole way of life. He served Guru Angad Dev Ji for thirteen years.

Every day he collected water from the Beas River for the Guru's bath. He was so devoted to the Guru that he would not even turn his back on him, so he walked backwards for the six-mile journey through forests to the river.

Guru Amar Das Ji became Guru when he was 73 years old. He encouraged the use of the **langar,** or Guru's kitchen, to carry on Guru Nanak Dev Ji's tradition of community eating. He also asked his followers to come to his headquarters in **Goindwal** three times a year on the dates of important Hindu festivals.

Guru Ram Das Ji (1574–1581)

Guru Ram Das Ji founded the sacred city of **Amritsar.** He was the son-in-law of Guru Amar Das Ji, and took over from him in 1574 at the age of 40. Guru Ram Das Ji invited people from 52 different trades to come to Amritsar and start new businesses in the "Guru's Market." He also composed the **Lavan,** which is a special hymn sung at Sikh weddings and a central part of the marriage service. He died at the age of 57.

Guru Arjan Dev Ji (1581–1606)

Guru Arjan Dev Ji was the fifth Guru, and the youngest son of Guru Ram Das Ji. Guru Arjan Dev Ji built the **Harimandir Sahib** at Amritsar, now called the Golden Temple, in the middle of the lake constructed by the fourth Guru. He also built **gurdwaras** (temples) at the great cities of Tarn Taran, Kartarpur, and Shri Hargobindpur.

The Golden Temple at Amritsar

Guru Gobind Singh Ji, with his characteristic baaj, *or hawk*

Guru Arjan Dev Ji collected together the hymns of the first four Gurus, along with some of his own, in a volume called the **Adi Granth.** Sikhs believe that the Gurus' hymns are the words of God and, therefore, these holy scriptures are treated with utmost respect. Once the Adi Granth was completed and placed in the Harimandir, Guru Arjan Dev Ji slept on the floor of the temple, to show his love and respect for the word of God.

Guru Arjan Dev Ji was the first Sikh martyr. The Mogul emperor Jehangir was jealous of the Guru's fame and following. Even some devout Muslims were praising the Guru's saintliness. At his court, Jehangir tried to convert Guru Arjan Dev Ji to Islam under the threat of death.

Guru Arjan Dev Ji refused, and was tortured and martyred. The torture lasted for five days. The Guru was first placed in a tank of boiling water. The next day, he had to sit on a plate of red-hot iron. On the third day, red-hot sand was poured over his blistered body. Guru Arjan Dev Ji remained calm and peaceful throughout his ordeal to show that all people should happily accept the will of God. Before his death, Guru Arjan Dev Ji sent a message that his son Har Gobind was to become the sixth Guru. He said that as peaceful means had failed with the Emperor, it was now right to use the sword to protect the weak and innocent, so he instructed Guru Har Gobind Ji to carry weapons.

Developing Sikhism

The next four Gurus are remembered because of the contributions they made towards the development of Sikhism.

Guru Angad Dev Ji began the collection of hymns that would later form the **Guru Granth Sahib Ji** and taught his followers that sports were necessary in order to develop a healthy body, which was as important to God as a healthy mind. After the death of Guru Angad Dev Ji, all the Gurus who succeeded were from the Sodhi family of Guru Amar Das Ji.

Guru Amar Das Ji strengthened Guru Nanak Dev Ji's teaching about community dining in the langar, which is central to Sikh belief.

Guru Ram Das Ji founded the city of Amritsar and composed the Lavan—the wedding hymn.

Guru Arjan Dev Ji (1581–1606) extended the collection of hymns begun by Guru Angad Dev Ji. He is remembered as the first Sikh martyr. Guru Arjan Dev Ji was also responsible for building the Harimandir Sahib in Amritsar—also known as the Darbar Sahib, or "Sacred Audience"—in 1604. He designed the temple so that everyone had to step down to enter it, and gave it entrances on all four sides to show that it was open to people of every religion or **caste**. The foundation stone of the temple was laid by by a Muslim holy man from Lahore called Mian Mir.

The Gurus 2

In this section you will:

- ● learn about the lives of some more of the Sikh Gurus and their influence on Sikhism;
- ● learn about the teachings of these Gurus.

Guru Har Gobind Ji (1606–1644)

Guru Har Gobind Ji was the only son of Guru Arjan Dev Ji. He was eleven years old when his father was executed and he became the sixth Guru.

Guru Har Gobind Ji is sometimes called the Warrior Guru because, after his father's death, instead of wearing the traditional prayer beads, he wore two **kirpans,** or swords. One sword represented spiritual power, and the other worldly power. These two swords appeared on the flags of his army and are now on the Sikh flag, the **Nishan Sahib.**

Guru Har Gobind Ji trained **Sikhs** to fight in order to defend themselves if necessary. He had a small army and fought against the Mogul emperor on several occasions. Even today some Sikhs in India still wear the "warrior uniform."

Guru Har Rai Ji (1644–1661)

Guru Har Rai Ji was fourteen years old when he became the seventh Guru. His father instructed him that he should always have 2,200 soldiers and horses with him.

Guru Har Rai Ji is also remembered for setting up a system to give free medicines to the sick. Today, some of the large **gurdwaras** in India continue to give free medical treatment to the poor.

Guru Har Rai Ji

Sikhs holding the Nishan Sahib

The Emperor of India asked Guru Har Rai Ji to come and explain his hymns. He sent his son, Ram Rai, instead, instructing him that not one word of the hymns could be changed because they were the words of God. However, Ram Rai was tested by the Emperor and finally broke the rule his father had given him. Because of this, Guru Har Rai Ji declared that the next Guru would be his youngest son, Har Krishan.

Guru Har Krishan Ji (1661–1664)

Guru Har Krishan Ji was only five years old when he succeeded his father, so he is sometimes called the "Child Guru." He died of smallpox at the age of eight and named his great uncle as his successor. While he was dying, it is said, many people who also had smallpox were healed when they drank spring water that he gave them.

There is a famous gurdwara called Bangla Sahib at the site of Guru Har Krishan Ji's place of death in Delhi.

Guru Tegh Bahadur Ji (1664–1675)

Guru Tegh Bahadur Ji was given his name, which means "brave sword," to replace his birth name Tyag Mal. He was the youngest son of Guru Har Gobind Ji.

Many people plotted against Guru Tegh Bahadur Ji. He fought against the Mogul rulers who were destroying Sikh temples and forcing people to convert to Islam. The Emperor had made Sikhs and Hindus pay large taxes, and had closed their schools and temples. Guru Tegh Bahadur Ji resisted the Emperor and was arrested.

Four of the Guru's companions were executed while he was made to watch because they would not convert to Islam. Then he was also killed.

Guru Tegh Bahadur Ji is respected by Sikhs especially because he died protecting the liberty of both Sikhs and Hindus. He was 54 years old when he died, and a gurdwara called Sis Ganj Sahib now stands in the square in Delhi where he was executed.

Peace and strife

Guru Har Gobind Ji established a court at the Akal Takht in Amritsar. He was imprisoned twice by Mogul rulers and had to spend the end of his life in Kiratpur in the foothills of the Himalayas.

Guru Har Rai Ji was a man of peace who spent his time in prayer and knew very little about fighting. He made the mistake of helping Dara Shikoh, who was leading a revolt against his brother Aurangzeb, the Mogul emperor. He said that, as a true Sikh, he had simply helped a man who needed help. When Guru Har Rai Ji sent his son to represent him at the Mogul court, Ram Rai is said to have performed miracles and altered a line of the **Adi Granth** to please the emperor.

When Guru Har Rai Ji chose Guru Har Krishan Ji as the next Guru, Ram Rai asked the Mogul emperor for help. The boy was called to Delhi and arrived there during a severe cholera epidemic. Although he cured many people, he died of smallpox. His last words were "Baba Bakale," meaning that the next Guru would be found in the village of Bakala.

Guru Tegh Bahadur Ji was a very successful preacher and converted many people to Sikhism. Because of this, he was executed by the Moguls.

Guru Gobind Singh Ji

In this section you will:

- learn about the life of Guru Gobind Singh Ji;
- learn about the teachings of Guru Gobind Singh Ji;
- read about the varied skills of Guru Gobind Singh Ji.

Guru Gobind Singh Ji (1666–1708)

Guru Gobind Singh Ji was nine years old when his father Guru Tegh Bahadur Ji was executed and he had to take on the role of Guru. He was the last human Guru, and probably the most famous after **Guru Nanak Dev Ji.**

Guru Gobind Rai Ji, as he was originally known, was a very clever linguist and a skilled horseman, archer, and hunter. He was also a great poet, and a book of his poems called the **Dasam Granth** (the Tenth Collection) is second in importance to the **Guru Granth Sahib Ji** itself.

Guru Gobind Rai Ji is remembered for two very important contributions to Sikhism.

He formed the **Khalsa,** the "community of the pure," and he chose the **Adi Granth,** now called the Guru Granth Sahib Ji, to succeed him and to be the final authority or Guru.

The Khalsa

In 1699 **Sikhs** from all over the Punjab were gathered at Anandpur, which is in a valley at the foot of the Himalayas, to follow the instructions of Guru Amar Das Ji. This was during **Baisakhi,** the Hindu festival of the wheat harvest, which is celebrated on April 13 (or on April 14 once every 36 years).

Guru Gobind Rai Ji gave a new meaning to Baisakhi for Sikhs. He asked for five volunteers who would give up their life for their faith. Each man went into a tent and the Guru then came out with blood on his sword. After the fifth man had gone inside, the tent was opened to show that all five were alive and well.

These men, the **panj piare,** or "'Five Beloved Ones," had been prepared to die for their faith. This event marked the founding of the Khalsa— the community of the pure. From now on, all Sikhs were encouraged to wear the **panj kakke**—five Ks. Guru Gobind Rai Ji also said that all Sikh males should take the name **Singh,** meaning "lion," and that Sikh females should take the name **Kaur,** which means "princess." He then changed his name to Guru Gobind Singh Ji. He dissolved sugar crystals in water, stirring with a **khanda** (a double-edged sword). Then he sprinkled this water over the panj piare.

Guru Gobind Singh Ji with his sons

The Guru Granth Sahib Ji is the final Sikh Guru.

The events at Baisakhi in 1699 marked the founding of the Khalsa and since then, the festival of Baisakhi has been the beginning of the Sikh New Year.

Guru Gobind Singh Ji and his followers in Anandpur were constantly under attack from the Mogul armies, and he and his wife were forced to leave. Many battles were fought between the Khalsa and the Moguls. During these battles, Guru Gobind Singh Ji lost his four sons and his mother. Countless numbers of Sikhs were killed, but this did not stop more and more Sikhs from joining the ranks of the Khalsa. Guru Gobind Singh Ji died of war wounds in 1708.

The Guru Granth Sahib Ji

When he was lying on his death bed, Guru Gobind Singh Ji took five coins and a coconut. He placed these in front of the Adi Granth. This was the way in which a new Guru was given office, and so by doing this, he was naming the Adi Granth as his successor. From then on, the Adi Granth was known as the Guru Granth Sahib Ji.

Soldier and poet

Guru Gobind Singh Ji was a great soldier and scholar. He also spoke Persian, Arabic, Sanskrit, and Punjabi. He improved Sikh law and was the author of the Dasma Granth—the Tenth Volume. Possibly his greatest achievement was creating a strong military base for the Sikhs of the Punjab.

He wrote poetry and music to urge his soldiers on, and created a love of the sword, which he called his "sacrament of steel."

He attacked the enemies of the Sikhs by sending one army against the Mogul empire and another against the hill tribes. All his soldiers were totally committed to fighting for the ideals of Sikhism, and to gain religious and political freedom for Sikhs so that they could again live in peace.

In a battle near Ambala, Guru Gobind Singh Ji lost all of his four sons and, later, his wife and mother. The Guru himself was killed by a Pashtun tribesman in revenge for the death of the man's own father.

Sikh Leaders

In this section you will:

- learn about leaders in Sikhism;
- find out about the work of the granthi in the gurdwara.

There are no priests in Sikhism as in some other religions, but there is a person who is responsible for leading the services.

Anyone who is a member of the **Khalsa** can read from the **Guru Granth Sahib Ji,** but it is usual for a **gurdwara** to have a person who is specially trained to read from Guru Granth Sahib Ji. This person is called a **granthi,** or "reader," and can be either a man or a woman. The granthi is also responsible for looking after the Guru Granth Sahib Ji.

In some gurdwaras, the granthi is employed full time and this is funded by the local community. In larger gurdwaras the granthi works for the gurdwara full time. In small villages in the Punjab and elsewhere, most granthis work part-time and have other jobs.

As well as reading from the Guru Granth Sahib Ji, the granthi is also responsible for organizing the ceremonies in the gurdwara.

However, even when there is a full-time granthi, other people may read from the Guru Granth Sahib Ji and may also lead the worship and the singing.

In addition to being responsible for worship in the gurdwara, some granthis may visit the sick and needy and comfort those who are mourning a death. However, even when there is a granthi, these duties also belong to the entire **Sikh** community.

A granthi reading from the Guru Granth Sahib Ji

Ragis perform an important role in the gurdwara.

Along with the granthi, the **ragi** is also an important person in the gurdwara. During services, a ragi sits to the side of the Guru Granth Sahib Ji and provides music for singing. The most common instruments are the baja, which is like a harmonium or reed organ, and a tabla or jorri, which is a drum.

Granthis

Unlike many other religions, there are no priests in Sikhism and any member of the Khalsa can read from the Guru Granth Sahib Ji. People who are specially trained to do this are called granthi. Anyone, male or female, can become a granthi and can take on the responsibility of leading worship. In some religions, such as Christianity, the religious leaders are priests or ministers, and can perform special services and rites, such as baptisms and confirmations.

A granthi's duties

The granthi plays a key role in the life of a gurdwara. It is the responsibility of the granthi to look after the Guru Granth Sahib Ji, the Sikh scriptures, and to see that it is laid to rest each night and brought from its own room to the prayer hall each morning.

Sikh Beliefs About God

In this section you will:
- learn what Sikhs believe about God;
- learn about the Mool Mantar;
- read about nammarga—"the way of nam."

The Mool Mantar

One of the central statements of **Sikh** belief is in a short hymn called the **Mool Mantar.** "Mool Mantar" means basic teaching, and is found at the beginning of the **Guru Granth Sahib Ji.** It is repeated each day during early morning prayer. The first words of the Mool Mantar are **Ik Onkar,** meaning "There is only One God."

The symbol for Ik Onkar is seen in many places such as badges, on the walls of a **gurdwara,** and in the home. It is a constant reminder to Sikhs of their faith and belief in **Waheguru.**

The Mool Mantar is a key statement of Sikh beliefs.

The Mool Mantar

Ik Onkar	There is only One God
Sat Nam	Eternal truth is God's name
Karta Purakh	God is the creator
Nir Bhau	God is without fear
Nir Vair	God is without hate
Akal Murat	Immortal, without form
Ajuni	Beyond birth and death
Saibhang	God is the enlightener
Gur Parshad	God can be reached through the mercy and grace of the true **Guru**

Beliefs about God

The most important belief in Sikhism is that there is only one God, Waheguru, and that God is beyond the understanding of human beings. God cannot be described, because description in human terms will always be less than what God is. God is neither male nor female. God is the creator who created the world for people to use and enjoy. God is everywhere and beyond everything. However, God created people and made them so that they would know the difference between right and wrong. Although people may know the difference between right and wrong, they still have to choose the right path for themselves. God is present in everyone's soul, according to Sikhism, but can only be seen by those who are blessed. God is personal and is available to everyone.

Sikhs believe that their one God is the God of all religions. No one religion can claim to be the only true way to God, and different religions are just different ways to God. So, it is not important which God people worship, but that they follow God's teachings so that they have the chance of achieving **mukti,** or escape from rebirth.

You are Father, Mother, Friend, Brother; with you as support everywhere, what fear can I have?

Guru Granth Sahib Ji

> There are many Sikh names for God, such as:
>
> Sat Nam   Eternal Reality
>
> Akal Purakh   Eternal One
>
> Waheguru   Wonderful Lord

One important Sikh belief is that Sikhs should keep the name of God in their minds and live their lives as God would wish. To do this many Sikhs practice **Nam Japna** throughout the day by repeating the word "Waheguru" under their breath.

Nammarga

Sikhism is sometimes called nammarga— "the way of nam"—because one of the important parts of Sikh worship is to repeat "Japna," a name for God. Sikhs believe that repeating God's name helps to free them from any sin they have done and to conquer evil thoughts. Once they have reached this stage, they can then work to overcome anger, attachment, greed, lust, and pride. Nam Japna—saying Waheguru, or "Wonderful Lord"—helps Sikhs to concentrate and to become still in their thoughts. In this way, they can begin to open the dasam duar, the "tenth gate," which leads to mukti and escape from rebirth.

Sikhism teaches that there is only one God. The statement, "Ik Onkar," is the opening line of the Mool Mantar: "God is the Truth, the Creator, immortal, and omnipresent. God has no form and is beyond human understanding." Mool Mantar means basic teaching, and it is recited at morning prayer each day.

Ik Onkar—the first words of the Mool Mantar

Sikh Beliefs About Life

In this section you will:

● learn what Sikhs believe about how they should live their lives;

● find out about mukti;

● read about Sikh's beliefs about reincarnation.

Sikhs believe that everything that happens is **Hukam,** the will of God. They belive that there is a divine spark—a part of God—in each person and that this spark, or soul, is taken back to God when a person reaches **mukti** and is finally released from the cycle of rebirth.

Sikhs believe that there are nearly eight and a half million different forms of life, and that many souls have to travel though a large number of these before they can finally reach God, or **Waheguru.** Each time something dies, the soul is reborn. It is only humans who can know the difference between right and wrong, and so it is only when the soul is in a human being that the cycle can be broken.

Sikhs believe that the ten **Gurus** had already reached a stage in life where they did not need to be reborn, but that they were sent back to earth to become God's messengers and lead other people to Waheguru**.**

Karma—actions and the consequences of these actions—decide whether a soul can be set free from the cycle. Freedom from this cycle is called mukti.

In Sikhism, there are several things, or influences, that can stop a soul from reaching mukti:

● a hankar—pride;

● kam—lust or desire;

● karodh—anger;

● lobh—greed;

Prayer is an important element of Sikh worship.

Sikhs believe in hard work and helping others.

- moh—being too attached to the world;

- **manmukh**—being self-centered instead of God-centered (**gurmukh**);

- maya—delusion, that is, looking at the world and ignoring God.

Those who live without these influences or dangers devote their life to **sewa**—selfless service to others.

To avoid those dangers, Sikhs are encouraged to follow these rules of conduct:

- There is only one God. Worship and pray to God alone, and remember God at all times.

- Always work hard, and share with others.

- Live a truthful life.

- Remember that men and women are equal in God's eyes.

- The whole human race is one. Distinctions of **caste,** color, class, and religion are wrong.

- Idols, magic, omens, fasts, marks on the face, and sacred threads are banned.

- Dress simply and modestly.

- **Khalsa** Sikh women should not wear the veil. Neither women nor men should make holes in their ears and noses.

- Live a married life.

- Put your faith in the **Guru Granth Sahib Ji.**

- Avoid lust, anger, greed, attachment to worldly things, and arrogance.

- Live a humble and simple life.

Reincarnation

Several Eastern religions, such as Buddhism and Hinduism, teach the doctrine of reincarnation. This belief says that a soul may be reborn many times into different forms of life. The form of life into which the soul is reborn will depend on the behavior of the soul in its previous life. Sometimes, a soul can make its way up through various life forms but, on other occasions, it may go backwards. Sikhism teaches that it is only by being born as a human being that the soul has a real chance of being finally free to join God—Waheguru—because only humans have the ability to know the difference between right and wrong, and so to choose the correct way of life.

To reach mukti, or freedom, is the aim of all Sikhs. This is not because they do not enjoy their lives, but because they want to be released from the cycle of rebirth so that the divine spark that is in all life can join God.

Signs and Symbols 1

In this section you will:

● learn what is meant by the five Ks;

● learn about the symbolism of the five Ks;

● read about how wearing the five Ks might affect people's lives.

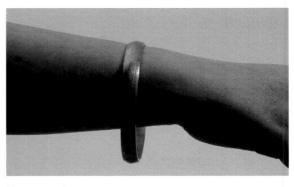

Kara

Symbols are a way in which we remind ourselves, and other people, of important ideas and beliefs. Signs and symbols are used in everyday life, and many religions have particular symbols of their own.

There are a number of important symbols in Sikhism.

In the past, a wider version of the kara was worn to protect the warrior's sword arm during a battle.

Kangha

The kangha is a comb used by Sikhs to keep their hair clean and tidy. When Guru Gobind Singh Ji founded the Khalsa he emphasized the importance of cleanliness. Sikhs are therefore encouraged to wash their hair early each morning. They then comb it and wind it into a topknot. The kangha is placed in the topknot to keep it in place. Sometimes the kangha has a small image of a **kirpan** (sword) on it. Using the khanga to keep their hair in place also reminds Sikhs of the need for discipline in order to live according to God's will.

The five Ks

Sikhs who are members of the **Khalsa** (the community of the "pure") are required to wear five symbols: **kara, kangha, kesh, kachera,** and **kirpan.** These **five Ks,** or **panj kakke,** show that the person is a Sikh. They also have spiritual meanings and are symbols of the faith. They have their origins in the establishment of the Khalsa by **Guru** Gobind Singh Ji at **Baisakhi** in 1699, and they remind Sikhs of their beliefs and their history.

Kara

The kara is a bracelet, made of iron or steel, never silver or gold, which is worn on the right wrist. Some Sikhs wear two karas. The metal is a symbol of strength, and the circle is a symbol of unity and eternity because a circle has no beginning and no end. This symbolizes the Sikh view of God, who is believed to be eternal and infinite. The circular shape also stands for the unity among Sikhs and between Sikhs and God.

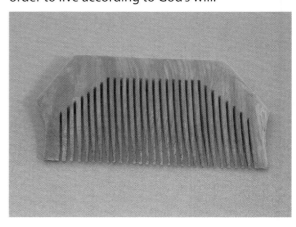

Kangha

Kesh

Kesh

Kesh is uncut hair. Guru Gobind Singh Ji told Khalsa Sikhs not to cut their hair, saying that it should be allowed to grow as God intended it to. Many Sikh men keep their hair covered with a **turban.** Young boys whose hair has not yet grown long enough for a turban may wear a small cloth over their topknot to keep their hair clean.

The five Ks

Signs and symbols are an important part of most religions, and also of life itself. We all use signs and symbols, often as a type of shorthand, and also as a reminder of a particular thing or idea. Signs and symbols are also useful because they can often reach across languages and cultures.

The five Ks are a very important aspect of Sikh life because they act as a constant reminder to Sikhs of who they are and what they believe in. They are first mentioned in the Rahatnamal, a writing by a follower of Guru Gobind Singh Ji.

Although the five Ks must be worn by Khalsa Sikhs, many other Sikhs choose to wear them as symbols of their religion.

Discrimination

Sometimes Sikhs have suffered discrimination because of wearing some of the five Ks. The most problematic is kesh, or uncut hair. Any Khalsa Sikh who cuts his or her hair is a *patit*, or renegade. Many Sikhs wear turbans, which are traditional in the Punjab, and which help to keep the hair clean and tidy. It is often the wearing of turbans that has caused Sikhs to be the victims of racism.

21

Signs and Symbols 2

In this section you will:

- learn about the kachera, the kirpan, and other Sikh symbols;
- learn about the importance of these symbols;
- read about the Nishan Sahib.

Kachera

Kachera are short trousers that are usually worn as undergarments. They are worn by men and women. **Guru** Gobind Singh Ji said that **Sikhs** should wear these short trousers as part of the **Khalsa** uniform. This may originally have been to distinguish Sikhs from Hindus, who traditionally wore dhotis (long loin cloths) or long cloaks. Both of these Hindu garments were unsuitable for fighting in and the kachera may have made it easier for Sikhs to fight in a battle if they had to do so.

Wearing these clothes reminds Sikhs that they must always be prepared to defend their religion and the rights of other people to practice their own faith. Today, these short trousers are seen as a symbol of modesty for many Sikhs and remind them of the need to live a good life according to the teachings of the Gurus.

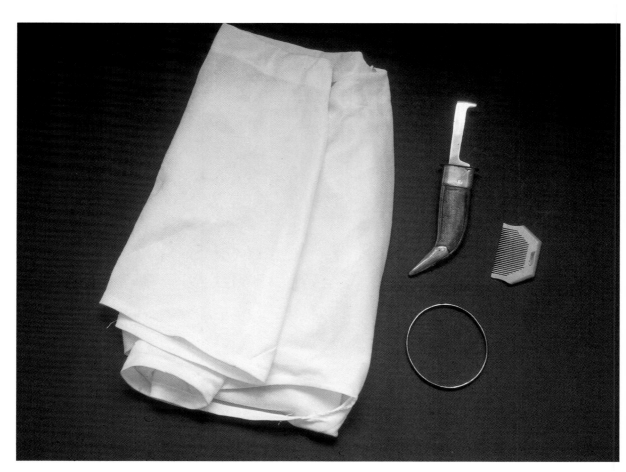

Kachera, kangha, kara, and kirpan

Kirpan

The **kirpan** is a sword worn by members of the Khalsa. The kirpan is worn as a reminder of the courage of the first five Sikhs, the **panj piare,** who were willing to let Guru Gobind Singh Ji cut off their heads with a kirpan for the sake of their religion. So it is a symbol of bravery and of faith in God. There was a time, however, when Sikhs were persecuted by the Mogul emperors, and they had to be ready to defend not only themselves, but also their faith. The kirpan is worn as a symbol of the Sikh being willing to defend his or her faith, or to defend the weak or oppressed.

Taking the kirpan out of its sheath would be considered disrespectful by some Sikhs. The kirpan is worn on a belt, which goes across the shoulder under a coat. Because the kirpan is seen as a weapon, Sikhs outside of the Punjab have sometimes been told that they are not allowed to wear it in public. They have objected to the kirpan being called a dagger or a knife because this suggests that they are carrying it as a weapon. Sometimes the kirpan is worn as a very small symbol on the **kangha.**

Nishan Sahib

The Sikh flag and symbol is called the **Nishan Sahib**. This flag always flies outside a **gurdwara.** It is a triangle of saffron or orange cloth. On the flag is the **khanda.** The khanda itself has three important symbols on it. The first is a double-edged sword (also known as a khanda), which is used to stir **amrit** in gurdwara services. The second is the **kara** (circular bracelet), given to Sikhs as a symbol of their unity and oneness with God. The third is two kirpans. The two kirpans represent spiritual power and worldly power, and were first carried by Guru Har Gobind Ji.

The flag is treated with great respect and is renewed each year at the festival of **Baisakhi.**

Ik Onkar

The first words of the **Mool Mantar** are **Ik Onkar,** meaning "There is only one God." The symbol for Ik Onkar (see page 17) is seen in many places, such as on badges, on the walls of a gurdwara, and in the home. It is there as a constant reminder to Sikhs of their belief in one God, **Waheguru.**

The Nishan Sahib

The Nishan Sahib flies outside of every gurdwara. It shows that the building is a gurdwara, in the same way as a cross is used on a church and the Star of David on a synagogue. It also represents a statement of a number of important Sikh beliefs.

The flag is triangular, and made of orange or saffron cloth. In the middle of the flag is the khanda. This shows some of the basic ideas of Sikhism. The double-edged sword is in the middle and represents Divine Knowledge—the sharp edges of the sword separate truth from lies. The kara or Chakar that surrounds the Khanda stands for the perfection of the eternal God, Waheguru. Finally, the two curved kirpans represent Miri—temporal authority, and Piri—spiritual authority. These two swords were first introduced by Guru Hargobind Dev Ji and show that Sikhs must be concerned with the practical needs of society as well as the spiritual life. At the top of the flagpole is a khanda, or spear, which is covered with the same cloth as the flag.

The Gurdwara

In this section you will:

- read about the gurdwara and its place in the Sikh community;
- learn about the importance of these buildings.

Gurdwara means "the doorway of the **Guru.**" It is a building in which the **Sikh** holy book, the **Guru Granth Sahib Ji,** is kept, and it is a place where Sikhs worship together. A gurdwara is also a community center for Sikhs where they have the opportunity to meet other Sikhs and also to worship together.

Gurdwaras are particularly important in Sikh communities outside of the Punjab, because in other countries, Sikhs may not live close to other Sikh families.

Outside a gurdwara there are usually symbols to show what it is. There is a flagpole flying the **Nishan Sahib,** the Sikh flag. This is triangular, orange or saffron in color, and on it is a symbol known as the **khanda.** This consists of two curved **kirpans** (swords), a khanda (double-edged sword) and a **kara** (circular bangle).

Shoes must not be worn in the main prayer hall of a gurdwara. There are also sinks so that people can wash their hands before worship, and a box of head coverings for non-Khalsa Sikhs, because people must cover their heads as a sign of respect. Anyone is welcome in a gurdwara as long as they have no traces of alcohol or tobacco on them.

In the main prayer hall there is a large carpeted area. There are no seats or chairs because the **sadhsangat** (congregation) sit on the floor cross-legged. Feet must not point toward the Guru Granth Sahib Ji. Women and men sit on opposite sides of the gurdwara in order not to distract each other during worship.

Sikhs in a gurdwara, the central place of Sikh community worship

The Guru Granth Sahib Ji is laid to rest for the night.

At one end of the hall is the **manji sahib** (a raised platform) with a **chanani** (canopy). There are cushions on the manji with **romalla** (decorative cloths) draped over them. The romalla cover the Guru Granth Sahib Ji when it is not being read. This is the daytime resting place of the Guru Granth Sahib Ji. The **granthi,** who may be a man or a woman, sits behind the Guru Granth Sahib Ji, facing the worshipers. In front of the manji sahib there is a long box called a **golak,** in which worshipers place their money offerings.

There is another platform where the **ragis** (musicians) sit to play their instruments during **kirtan** (hymn singing). Music is an important aspect of Sikh worship as an accompaniment to the singing of the scriptures. Verses from the scriptures are set to music and are called **shabads,** or hymns. The hymns found in the Guru Granth Sahib Ji are known as **Gurbani,** which means "the words of the Guru."

It is important for Sikhs to remember the words of the shabads, but it is more important that they understand their meaning. Before a hymn is sung, the ragis will read it and will say a few words of explanation. Shabads are sung solemnly and slowly, and great care is taken to pronounce the words so that everyone can hear them clearly.

Inside a gurdwara there is a room that is the resting room for the holy scriptures. This room has a bed, with pillows, covers, and a canopy. The Guru Granth Sahib Ji is "put to bed" each night by the granthi or by another Sikh who says the **Kirtan Sohila** prayer. Each morning it is "awakened" and placed on the manji sahib.

Sikh places of worship

Every religion has particular places in which people come together to worship. The way in which these buildings are used may vary from one faith to another. The first Sikh place of worship was built at Kartapur by Guru Nanak Dev Ji, and was called *dharamsala*, a place of faith.

A gurdwara is any building where there is a copy of the Guru Granth Sahib Ji. The most important gurdwara is the **Harimandir Sahib,** the Golden Temple, in Amritsar, which was built by Guru Arjan Dev Ji to hold the first copy of the Guru Granth Sahib Ji. There are more than 200 historical gurdwaras in India, which have been built on particular sites associated with events in the life of one of ten gurus. Many of these are centers for **yatras,** or pilgrimage, during Sikh festivals.

Around the world, Sikh communities build local gurdwaras to provide homes for the Guru Granth Sahib Ji, and as centers for worship and community life. Some Sikhs set aside a room at home for a copy of the Guru Granth Sahib Ji, and so their houses become gurdwaras. Every large gurdwara also has a **langar,** where all visitors are asked to share in a common meal.

The Langar

In this section you will:
- learn about the langar;
- learn about importance of sharing and equality in Sikhism;
- read about the food and drink shared in the langar.

Every **gurdwara** has a **langar**—"**Guru's** kitchen" or eating area. The meal eaten here is also called a langar. The langar is part of the act of worship and is a very important aspect of **Sikh** life. There is no charge for the food served in the langar.

Guru Nanak Dev Ji started the custom of the langar because he rejected the Hindu **caste** system. In this system, people of different castes are not allowed to eat together. Guru Nanak Dev Ji wanted to stress the idea that everyone is equal, so he wanted everyone to be able to eat the same food in the langar regardless of social class, sex, religion, or caste. Also, everyone was to share the tasks of preparation, cooking, serving, and cleaning. This shows **sewa**—selfless service to others in the **sadhsangat,** the gurdwara, and the world outside. Sewa is a very important aspect of Sikhism. This teaching was reinforced by Guru Amar Das Ji, who made a rule that no one could see him until they had first eaten in the langar.

Sikh families consider it a privilege to provide for the langar and to serve others. There is usually a waiting list of people who want to provide the langar each week.

The food is usually served by the male members of the congregation. There are no special places to sit and everyone eats the same food. Although not all Sikhs are vegetarian, no meat is served in

Sharing food together in the langar illustrates the equality of all people before God.

Vegetarian food is served in the langar so that no one is excluded.

the langar so that no one will be excluded from the meal regardless of their religious dietary beliefs. Sikhs are not allowed to eat any meat that has been ritually slaughtered, such as that for Jews or Muslims.

Food is usually served on trays that have five or six compartments. These will probably contain food such as *chapatis* (flat bread), a vegetable curry, mixed salad, sweet rice or other sweet milk dishes, and pieces of fresh fruit.

Community dining

The first Sikh dining room was set up by Guru Nanak Dev Ji at Mardana in Sultanpur. This practice of establishing a place in a gurdwara where everyone could eat together regardless of race, religion, or caste was continued by by the second guru, Guru Angad Dev Ji and, in particular, by the third guru, Guru Amar Das Ji. Guru Amar Das Ji would not see anyone who had not first eaten in the langar to show equality. Even the Mogul emperor Akbar ate there before visiting the Guru for his blessing.

Food and drink

Hindus do not eat beef, and many Hindus are vegetarians. Muslims and Jews do not eat pork. So, although Sikhs are not required to be vegetarian, no meat is served in the langar in order that everyone can share the same meal.

In the langar, everyone sits on the floor to be equal, and the food is cooked and served by volunteers. This food is available at all times. On special occasions, such as festivals, the tea served in the langar may be made with milk that has been flavored with spices such as cinnamon.

Worship 1

In this section you will:

- learn about the Sikh service of worship;
- learn about importance of this worship;
- read about customs related to the gurdwara.

There is no fixed day for worship in Sikhism, although Sunday is a popular day both in India and other countries. This is because it is a day when most people do not go to work. Some communities have their services daily, or in the evenings. Prayers are said every morning and evening in the **gurdwara,** but not all members of the local community attend these.

Congregational worship is called **diwan**, but this service is sometimes called **kirtan.** "Kirtan" means hymn-singing, because verses from the **Guru Granth Sahib Ji** are sung as part of the service.

The weekly service

After bathing, members of the **sadhsangat** remove their shoes, cover their heads and wash their hands before entering the prayer hall.

As they enter the prayer hall, **Sikhs** approach the **manji sahib** (platform) on which the Guru Granth Sahib Ji is placed. They kneel on their hands and knees and lower their heads until their foreheads touch the floor, as a sign of respect. Then they make an offering of money, flowers, or food, both for charity and for the use of the Sikh community.

Sikhs may then greet other members of the congregation by saying **Waheguru** before taking up their places, sitting cross-legged on the floor facing the manji sahib. It is traditional for men and women to sit on opposite sides of the prayer hall.

The service may last for two hours or more. It begins early in the morning when the Guru Granth Sahib Ji is removed from its resting place

Sikhs kneel in front of the Guru Granth Sahib Ji.

The Ardas is an important Sikh prayer.

and set up on the manji sahib. There are readings from the Guru Granth Sahib Ji until the **ragis** (musicians) arrive. The readings are chosen at random.

The worshipers chant verses from the Guru Granth Sahib Ji, and the ragis sing and accompany them on musical instruments. The congregation joins in some of the hymns. This is the part of the service called kirtan.

Near the end of the service, a sermon is given by a member of the Sikh community. This is usually an explanation of the readings from the Guru Granth Sahib Ji.

At the end of the service there is a series of prayers that includes six verses from the **Anand Sahib,** a hymn written by Guru Amar Das Ji, the last part of the **Japji Sahib,** written by **Guru Nanak Dev Ji,** a verse from a hymn by Guru Arjan Dev Ji, and, finally, **Ardas.**

When Ardas is said, members of the congregation stand and face the Guru Granth Sahib Ji with the palms of their hands together as a mark of respect. The first part of Ardas mentions God and all the Gurus. The second part reminds Sikhs that the Guru Granth Sahib Ji is God's word and that of the faithful Sikhs of the past. The final part of Ardas is a prayer asking God to keep the **Khalsa** faithful and for the well-being of people of all races and religions.

While Ardas is being said, someone in the congregation prepares the **karah parshad** (a sweet food that is shared by the congregation), stirring it with a **kirpan,** After Ardas, everyone sits down. The karah parshad is offered first to five practicing Sikhs, in memory of the **panj piare,** and then passed out by placing in the hands of everyone present. This shared food shows that everyone is equal before God.

In the gurdwara

When a person goes into a gurdwara, they are expected to remove their shoes and to cover their head as a sign of respect to the Guru Granth Sahib Ji. People wash their hands and, sometimes, their feet as well. As worshipers approach the Guru Granth Sahib Ji, they bow down and touch the floor. The offerings that people make when they enter the gurdwara are voluntary.

Everyone sits on the floor so that the Guru Granth Sahib Ji is higher than everyone else. Although men and women traditionally sit separately, they are both at the same distance from the Guru Granth Sahib Ji.

People can enter or leave the gurdwara at any time during the service, but everyone is expected to stand facing the Guru Granth Sahib Ji when the Ardas is read.

The two most important aspects of worship in the gurdwara are kirtan, which is singing hymns from the Guru Granth Sahib Ji, and **katha,** which is reading and explaining texts from the Guru Granth Sahib Ji.

The distribution of karah parshad to everyone at the end of the service again stresses the Sikh teaching about equality.

Worship 2

In this section you will:
- learn about Sikh daily worship;
- learn about the importance of this worship;
- read about the Akhand Path and its history.

Mala—prayer beads

Nam Simran

Guru Nanak Dev Ji taught that the most important form of worship is **bhakti** (devotion to God). Some Sikhs say that the whole of Sikhism is bhakti.

When **Sikhs** meditate on the name of God, this is known as **Nam Simran** (thinking of the name). In this way, people sense God within themselves and grow ever closer to God.

Sikhs remember the presence of God through **Nam Japna,** a constant repetition of the name of God, "**Waheguru.**" This can be said aloud or silently.

Morning prayer

After bathing, meditate upon the Lord and your body and mind will become pure.

Guru Granth Sahib Ji

Guru Ram Das Ji said:

He who calls himself a Sikh of the great Sat Guru should rise early and meditate on God's name.

Guru Granth Sahib Ji

Sikhs get up early each day to pray and to meditate. This is called **amritvela**. The early morning is peaceful and is a good time for prayer and meditation. First, they take a bath and get dressed, then, after covering their heads, they can begin prayer.

Prayer begins with the **Japji Sahib,** a hymn of 38 verses that comes from the first section of the **Guru Granth Sahib Ji.** The opening verses of the Japji Sahib are the **Mool Mantar.** After the Japji Sahib, other prayers are said and, if there is time, some Sikhs will read hymns from a collection called the **gutka.** At the end of prayers, Sikhs meditate. Some people use **mala** (prayer beads) to help them.

Sikhs do not have set prayer positions, such as kneeling or sitting. Prayers must not be said while doing other things and, ideally, should be done in a quiet place without any distractions.

Throughout the day, some Sikhs will often practice Nam Japna by repeating the word "Waheguru," usually under their breath.

Sikh women praying at home

Evening prayer

In the evening, there are set hymns and prayers. **Sodar Rahiras** is said before the evening meal. Just before going to bed, Sikhs will recite a small group of hymns called the **Kirtan Sohila.**

The Akhand Path

The **Akhand Path** is a continuous reading of the Guru Granth Sahib Ji, from beginning to end. It takes place on special occasions, such as a marriage, and also during **gurpurbs.**

The Akhand Path takes about 48 hours, and the reading can be done by family members or by a groups of **granthis.** After the reading is over, the Bhog ceremony takes place. The Guru Granth Sahib Ji is opened at random, and a hymn from the page is read. After this, **karah parshad** is given to everyone present.

History of the Akhand Path

The Akhand Path ceremony began in the eighteenth century C.E., when there were very few copies of Guru Granth Sahib Ji available. Many Sikhs were fighting for their religion at this time and were in hiding in the jungles. Whenever they could, they would gather together and listen to a continuous reading from the Guru Granth Sahib Ji, before that copy of the book was moved to another place to be read to other people.

The Guru Granth Sahib Ji

In this section you will:
- learn about the Guru Granth Sahib Ji and its relevance to Sikhs
- learn about respect shown to the Guru Granth Sahib Ji.

The **Guru Granth Sahib Ji** is the holy scriptures of the **Sikhs.** The book is written mainly in Punjabi, using the **Gurmukhi**—"from the mouth of the **Guru**"—script. Every printed copy of the Guru Granth Sahib Ji is exactly the same, with 1,430 pages. The Guru Granth Sahib Ji can be translated, but these translations are not used in Sikh worship.

The Guru Granth Sahib Ji is a collection of the teachings and hymns of **Guru Nanak Dev Ji** and five of the other Sikh Gurus. It is treated as a living Guru by Sikhs, as Guru Gobind Singh Ji instructed.

The second Guru, Guru Angad Dev Ji, wrote down the hymns of Guru Nanak Dev Ji. The third Guru, Guru Amar Das Ji, composed more hymns, including the **Anand Sahib** (Hymn of Bliss). The fourth Guru, Guru Ram Das Ji, composed the **Lavan,** the four verses that are sung at a wedding ceremony while the bride and groom walk around the holy book. The fifth Guru, Guru Arjan Dev Ji, brought all the hymns of the other Gurus into one single set of scriptures, known as the **Adi Granth.**

Guru Gobind Singh Ji added more hymns written by his father, Guru Tegh Bahadur Ji. He announced that, after his death, there would be no other living Guru, but that the scriptures

Reading from the Guru Granth Sahib Ji

A page of the Guru Granth Sahib Ji, written in Gurmukhi script
should now become the Guru.

The Adi Granth then became a "Guru," and was known as the Guru Granth Sahib Ji. "Sahib" is a word that is added to a name to show respect. The Guru Granth Sahib Ji is given the same respect that was shown to the human Gurus during their lifetimes.

At the beginning of each day, the **granthi** and other Sikhs form a procession to carry the Guru Granth Sahib Ji from its night-time resting place to its position in the main prayer hall of the **gurdwara** on the **manji sahib.**

The Guru Granth Sahib Ji is never placed on the ground and Sikhs never turn their backs on it.

While the Guru Granth Sahib Ji is being read, the granthi waves a special fan, called a **chauri,** over the pages of the book. This chauri has a long handle and is made from yak's hair. It is used in remembrance of a **pakha,** which was used by Sikhs walking with the Gurus to keep them cool in the hot areas of the Punjab.

The Guru Granth Sahib Ji is of very great importance for Sikhs, who believe that its message is **Gurbani,** the word of God.

Many Sikhs own a copy of the Guru Granth Sahib Ji and take care to show it respect. Some Sikh families have a copy of the **Dasam Granth,** poetry written by Guru Gobind Singh Ji and not included in the Guru Granth Sahib Ji or the sacred **Nit nem** (a prayer book) at home.

The word of God

The Guru Granth Sahib Ji is a unique work. It is different from the holy books of other religions because, as well as the writings of six of the Sikh Gurus, it contains works by people from other faiths. Sikhs always treat it with the greatest respect. However, Sikhs do not worship idols, and so the respect they show for the Guru Granth Sahib Ji is for the writings it contains, which they believe are Gurbani, the word of God.

Most of the writings are in Punjabi, but there are also hymns in Persian, medieval Hindi, Sanskrit, and Arabic. Each of the 1,430 pages has eighteen or nineteen lines of Gurmukhi—"from the mouth of the Guru"—script, which was developed by Guru Angad Dev Ji.

The hymns are arranged according to the tune to which they are sung, then by the type of poem and, finally, by the key in which they are sung. This pattern was developed by Guru Arjan Dev Ji.

Every copy of the Guru Granth Sahib Ji is identical, with exactly 1,430 pages.

Festivals 1

In this section you will:

● learn about some of the Sikh festivals;

● learn about how these festivals are celebrated;

● read about some of the main gurpurbs.

There are two different types of festivals in Sikhism.

1. Special holy days, which celebrate events in the lives of the **Gurus.** These are known as **gurpurbs,** or Gurus' remembrance days.

2. Other celebrations, which are held on the same days as some Hindu festivals. These are known as **melas.**

Sikhs also celebrate the anniversaries of great events in Sikh history, such as **Baisakhi,** the foundation of the **Khalsa** in 1699.

Gurpurbs

The gurpurbs are days that commemorate the births and deaths of the Gurus. Some of these are particularly important. The dates are usually set according to the Indian calendar (the first set of times below) but in recent years, most of them have been placed on fixed dates. They include:

● the martyrdom of Guru Arjan Dev Ji (May/June) (June 16);

● the installation of the **Guru Granth Sahib Ji** (August/early September);

● the birthday of **Guru Nanak Dev Ji** (November);

● the birthday of Guru Gobind Singh Ji (December) (January 5);

● the martyrdom of Guru Tegh Bahadur Ji (December) (November 24).

The Guru Granth Sahib Ji being carried through the streets at a gurpurb

Sikhs celebrating the birthday of Guru Nanak Dev Ji

Part of the celebration of a gurpurb is a complete reading of the Guru Granth Sahib Ji, called the **Akhand Path.** Sikhs come to the **gurdwara** on the last day of the Akhand Path to hear the last pages of the Guru Granth Sahib Ji.

In India these events are celebrated on the actual day on which they fall, but in other countries, where Sikh communities are smaller, they are usually celebrated on the closest Sunday. The Akhand Path begins on Friday and ends at the Sunday service.

In India, the Guru Granth Sahib Ji is traditionally carried through the streets in a procession with five men representing the **panj piare.**

Gurpurbs

Gurpurbs are important anniversaries associated with the lives of the Gurus. In most gurdwaras, there is usually a reading of the Akhand Path, ending on the actual day when the gurpurb is celebrated. There is also **kirtan** (hymn singing from from the Guru Granth Sahib Ji) and katha (lectures on Sikhism). In some gurdwaras, there is nagar kirtan, when the Guru Granth Sahib Ji is carried in procession by five Sikhs, who also carry the Nishan Sahib. Sometimes, free sweets and **langar** are also given to the general public.

Main gurpurbs

The most important of the gurpurbs are:

- The first installation of the Guru Granth Sahib Ji in the Golden Temple by Guru Arjan Dev Ji in August 1604;

- The birth of Guru Nanak Dev Ji on April 15, 1469, in the Western Punjab village of Talwandi;

- The birth of Guru Gobind Singh Ji on December 22, 1666, at Patna;

- The martyrdom of Guru Arjan Dev Ji on May 30, 1606, in the River Ravi;

- The martyrdom of Guru Tegh Bahadur Ji on November 11, 1675, in Delhi, by order of the Mogul emperor.

Festivals 2

In this section you will:
- learn about more of the Sikh festivals;
- learn about how these festivals are celebrated;
- read about the festivals of Sangrand and Maghi.

Changing the Nishan Sahib at Baisakhi

Mela

There are three major **Sikh** festivals that are held on the same day as Hindu festivals. They are:

- **Baisakhi;**
- **Divali Mela** ("**mela**" means " fair");
- **Hola Mohalla Mela.**

Guru Amar Das Ji said that Sikhs should come together for worship during Baisakhi and Divali Mela. Guru Gobind Singh Ji added Hola Mohalla Mela as another time when Sikhs should celebrate together. Celebrating these festivals together confirmed that Sikhs were a separate religious group and that they no longer celebrated the festivals as Hindus.

Baisakhi

Baisakhi is the month of the wheat harvest in the Punjab. The festival is on April 13 (on April 14 once every 36 years), and now marks the Sikh New Year.

In 1699, Guru Gobind Singh Ji founded the **Khalsa** at Baisakhi. Sikhs also remember 1919, when 400 Sikhs (many of them women and children) were killed by British soldiers who had been ordered to break up their Baisakhi gathering at Jallianwala Bagh in **Amritsar.**

The **Nishan Sahib,** the Sikh flag, is changed at Baisakhi. During the festival, the **Akhand Path** is read and initiation ceremonies (**amrit**) are held.

In Amritsar, Baisakhi is a great animal fair. In India, many Sikhs are farmers, so a livestock market is not unusual.

Because Baisakhi is associated with celebrations of the birth of **Khalsa,** today it is also being used as an occasion for making political speeches.

Divali Mela

Divali Mela is celebrated throughout India in the autumn, and marks the end of the rainy season.

Sikhs commemorate the story of Guru Har Gobind Ji who returned to Amritsar on Divali. He had been in prison while the Mogul Emperor tried to stop the growth of Sikhism. The Emperor was sick, and his doctors said that his illness was caused because he had imprisoned a man of God. Guru Har Gobind Ji was released, but he said that he would not go unless he could take 52 Hindu princes who were also in prison with him.

The Mogul Jehangir told the Guru that he would free as many princes as could hold on to his clothes as he walked through a narrow passage.

The Golden Temple during Divali Mela

Guru Har Gobind Ji made himself a coat with long tassels, and all the princes went with him.

Many Sikh homes are decorated with diyas (clay lamps), candles, and colored lights. There are special meals and firework displays. It is a time of rejoicing. People give sweets to their friends and relatives. Services are held in **gurdwaras,** and the Golden Temple in Amritsar is lit up.

Hola Mohalla Mela

In 1700, Guru Gobind Singh Ji held a three-day festival at **Anandpur.** This became a time for Sikhs to train as soldiers. Guru Gobind Singh Ji wanted to prepare them for any trouble that might come.

Hola Mohalla means "attack and counterattack."

Sangrand

The festival of Sangrand marks the time when the sun passes from one sign of the zodiac to the next. It is the start of each new month in the Indian calendar. Sangrand is announced in the gurdwaras by reading the Bara Maha, the Song of the Twelve Months, by Guru Arjan Dev Ji and, sometimes, the Bara Maha of **Guru Nanak Dev Ji.** Sangrand is otherwise no more important than any other day.

Maghi

The festival of Maghi takes place on the first day of Maghar Sangrant, which is in mid-January. Sikhs go to gurdwaras for **kirtan** to mark the martyrdom of the Forty Immortals. These were followers of Guru Gobind Singh Ji who had been deserters. They returned, however, to help him fight the Moguls and were killed. They were blessed by the Guru, who said that they had achieved **mukti** by their bravery. They were cremated at Muktsar, where the largest gathering takes place.

Pilgrimage 1

In this section you will:

● learn about Sikh pilgrimage;

● read about some of the places that Sikhs might visit;

● learn about Guru Nanak Dev Ji's approach to pilgrimage.

True pilgrimage consists of the contemplation of the name of God and the cultivation of inner knowledge.

Guru Granth Sahib Ji

There is no place of pilgrimage equal to the Gurus. The Guru alone is the pool of contentment. The Guru is the river from which pure water is obtained, by which the soil of evil understanding is washed away.

Guru Granth Sahib Ji

There are no special times for pilgrimage in Sikhism, but many **Sikhs** try to visit places associated with their religion. Sikhs believe that God is everywhere, and so no one place is more holy than another.

The **Gurus** taught that it was not important to make special journeys to visit holy places. The important aspect of Sikh life is living according to God's will.

The Punjab in India is the homeland of Sikhs. More than half of the people who live there are Sikhs, and the language they speak is Punjabi. Of the world population of more than 19 million Sikhs, 80 percent live in the Punjab. Sikhs who do not live in the Punjab may also visit the Golden Temple at **Amritsar** and other places associated with the Gurus and their lives. These visits are called **yatras.**

Harimandir Sahib, the Golden Temple, is a very important center of pilgrimage for Sikhs.

The Harimandir Sahib

The most popular place to go on a yatra is the **Harimandir Sahib,** the Golden Temple at Amritsar. "Harimandir" means "God's House," and "**Sahib**" is added to the names of people, places, and things to show how much they are respected.

The Harimandir Sahib is a very special **gurdwara.** The first Guru, **Guru Nanak Dev Ji,** chose the site, which he said was a place of great beauty, and he said that the fourth Guru would build there. Guru Ram Das Ji began to build a large pool there, which he filled with **amrit** (nectar) and named Amritsar. This sort of pool is called a **serovar.** His son, Guru Arjan Dev Ji, built the Harimandir Sahib on an island in the middle of the serovar, finishing the work in 1601.

The Harimandir Sahib has always been a major meeting place for Sikhs when they have been persecuted. When the Mogul emperors were in power, they destroyed the temple and filled in the serovar. A Sikh leader, Baba Deep Singh, led a group of Sikhs who destroyed the Mogul army and restored the temple. In 1740 the temple was being used by nonbelievers as a hall for dancing and drinking. Two Sikhs traveled from the south of India to kill the ruler of Amritsar and to restore the temple.

The dome and the upper walls of the Harimandir Sahib are covered in gold leaf. There is a door on each of the four walls facing east, west, north and south, to show that the Harimandir Sahib is open to everyone. A long marble walkway crosses the serovar to the west door of the Harimandir Sahib, while a wide promenade, called the Pakirama, runs around the pool. There are also rows of rooms where pilgrims can rest. The **langar** in the Harimandir Sahib is open every day and anyone can eat there. The langar provides daily food for many of the poor people of Amritsar.

True pilgrimage

Sikhism teaches that a true pilgrimage is found in thinking about the name of God, and so reaching a better understanding of life. To Sikhs, this is far more important than visiting special places. Because God is everywhere, no place can be any more holy than any other place. Therefore, the most important thing for a human being is to learn to live according to God's will, so that the soul can finally be free from rebirth and can join **Waheguru.**

Guru Nanak Dev Ji refused to take part in Hindu pilgrimages. In particular, he was opposed to people making pilgrimages to the Hindu sacred Ganges River. It was while Lehna, later to be Guru Angad Dev Ji, was on his way to the shrine of a Hindu goddess that he met Guru Nanak Dev Ji in 1532. Guru Nanak Dev Ji refused to go with Lehna, and it was then that Lehna decided to become his follower.

The Harimandir Sahib, or Golden Temple, at Amritsar in the Punjab, the most popular place for Sikhs to visit, has been attacked many times in its history. Although the **Akal Takht** has recently suffered extensive damage, the Harimandir Sahib survived needing only minor repairs.

Pilgrimage 2

In this section you will:

● learn about other places of pilgrimage;

● learn about why Sikhs may visit these places;

● read about four takhts in addition to the Akal Takht.

Akal Takht

Akal Takht, which means " Throne of the Eternal," faces the Golden Temple, the **Harimandir Sahib,** and was built by **Guru** Har Gobind Ji in 1609. The building is used by **Sikhs** for political meetings and is the meeting place of the **Khalsa,** The highest Sikh court meets at the Akal Takht to make decisions on behalf of` the whole Sikh community.

The building was destroyed in 1984, but has since been rebuilt.

The Akal Takht houses the most sacred copy of the **Guru Granth Sahib Ji.** Each day, at 5:00 A.M. in winter and 4:00 A.M. in summer, it is carried in a golden **palanquin** to the Harimandir. It is carried back to rest at 10:00 P.M. in winter and 11:00 P.M. in summer. Outside the building are two large flagpoles. One has the flag of Miri— earthly authority—and the other of Piri— spiritual authority.

Anandpur Sahib

Anandpur Sahib is another special place for Sikhs. It is in a valley at the foot of the Himalayas. The ashes of the head of Guru Tegh Bahadur Ji are buried there, and it is also the place where Guru Gobind Singh Ji founded the **Khalsa.** The most important celebrations for the festival of **Hola Mohalla Mela** take place at Anandpur.

Goindwal

Guru Amar Das Ji had a very deep well, or baoli, built at **Goindwal.** It provided safe drinking water and was surrounded by trees to improve the environment. It became a tradition for people to bathe in the well and, as people go down into it, they say the **Japji Sahib** on each of the 84 steps. Some people say that, by doing this, they will get nearer to **mukti.**

Pilgrimage, austerity [living simply], mercy, almsgiving, and charity bring merit, be it as little as a mustard seed; but those who hear, believe, and cherish the word, an inner pilgrimage and cleansing is theirs.

From the Japji Sahib

The Akal Takht is a central place for Sikh meetings.

The Gurus said that ceremonial bathing served no purpose. When people recite the Japji Sahib going down into the well, they do not benefit from the bathing. They benefit because they have meditated on God's name.

If someone goes to bathe at a place of pilgrimage with the mind of a crook and the body of a thief then his outside will have been washed but his inside will be dirty twice over…. The saints are good even without such washing. Thieves remain thieves even if they bathe at a place of pilgrimage.

Guru Granth Sahib Ji

Other takhts

There are four other takhts in addition to the Akal Takht.

Takht Sri Damdama Sahib is in the village of Talwandi Sabo near Bhatinda. Guru Gobind Singh Ji stayed here for a year in 1705, while he put together the final edition of the Guru Granth Sahib Ji, which was then known as the Damdama Sahib Bir.

Takht Sri Keshgarh Sahib is at Anandpur Sahib. The Khalsa was founded here by Guru Gobind Singh Ji in 1699, and some of the weapons he used are kept here. The most important of these is the actual **khanda** used by Guru Gobind Singh Ji to prepare the **amrit** during the first Khalsa initiation ceremony.

Takht Sri Hazur Sahib is in Maharashtra, on the banks of Godavari, and is where Guru Gobind Singh Ji died in 1708. The inner part of the temple is the Angitha Sahib, which stands over the site where Guru Gobind Singh Ji was cremated.

Takht Sri Patna Sahib is in Patna, the capital of Bihar. It is the birthplace of Guru Gobind Singh Ji. The Guru was born here in 1666, and spent his childhood here before moving to Anandpur. As well as being the birthplace of Guru Gobind Singh Ji, Patna was visited by **Guru Nanak Dev Ji** and Guru Tegh Bahadur Ji.

The entrance to the well at Goindwal

Growing Up

In this section you will:

- learn about Sikh birth and initiation ceremonies;
- learn how these ceremonies are observed;
- read about the ethical code which Khalsa Sikhs follow.

Birth

As soon as a baby is born, many **Sikhs** whisper the words of the **Mool Mantar** in his or her ear and place a drop of honey on his or her tongue.

The name-giving ceremony

Once the mother and child are well enough to go out, there is a special ceremony held at the **gurdwara.** Outside India, this usually happens during the regular weekly service.

The **granthi** opens the **Guru Granth Sahib Ji** at random. The baby's name will begin with the first letter of the first hymn on the left-hand side of the page. The parents have some time to choose a name. This name is announced by the granthi, who adds the title **Singh** for a boy or **Kaur** for a girl. The granthi then shouts "Jo bole so nihal" ("Whoever believes in the truth will be saved"), and the **Sadhsangat,** or congregation, reply, "Sat sri akahl"("The Truth is eternal").

The ceremony ends with the **Anand Sahib** (Hymn of Bliss), and **karah parshad** is given to the congregation.

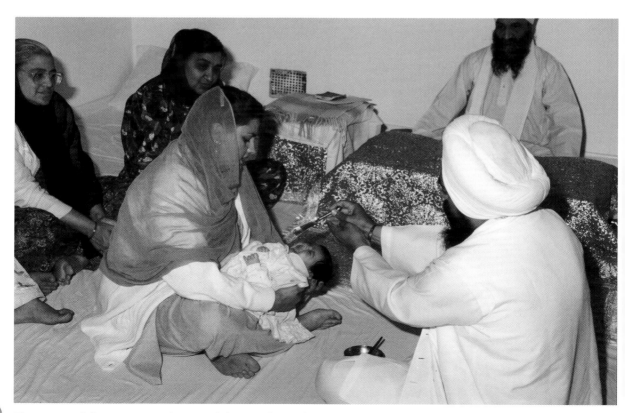

The name-giving ceremony is a special event that takes place in the gurdwara.

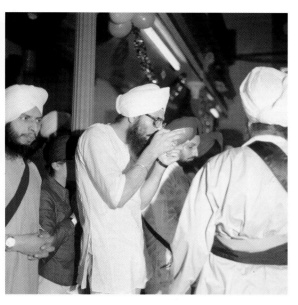

Hymns are sung from the Guru Granth Sahib Ji, the candidates drink amrit, and say these words: "The Khalsa is of God, the victory is to God." The amrit is sprinkled on the hair and eyes of the candidates five times, then the Mool Mantar is read and repeated. **Ardas** is said and karah parshad is distributed to everyone. Sikhs who do not join the Khalsa are called **Sahaj-dhari,** or "seekers after God."

The Amrit ceremony is the initiation ceremony for Khalsa Sikhs.

Initiation into the Khalsa

Boys and girls aged fourteen or sixteen are able to join the **Khalsa.** In order to join the Khalsa, Sikhs must have the **panj kakke,** the five Ks: **kesh** (uncut hair); **kangha** (a wooden comb); **kachera** (short trousers); **kirpan** (a short sword); and **kara** (an iron or steel bracelet).

The ceremony is called the **Amrit** ceremony, and is conducted by five members of the Sikh community, who are already members of the Khalsa, representing the **panj piare.** They wear ceremonial robes: knee-length tunics in orange or saffron, blue sashes around their waists and over the shoulder, and a blue or orange turban.

One of the five members of the Khalsa explains the principles of the Sikh faith and reminds the candidates of the teachings of the Guru Granth Sahib Ji. The candidates for initiation are asked if they accept these principles. The five members of the Khalsa then kneel around an iron bowl, and prepare amrit from sugar and water. The bowl represents strength. The water represents the source of life. Sikhs believe that once this water has been blessed it purifies the soul. The liquid is stirred with a **khanda** (a double-edged sword).

An ethical code

Members of the Khalsa live according to an ethical code, the Reht Maryada:

Sikhs will worship only God.

Sikhs must put their faith in the Guru Granth Sahib Ji.

Sikhs do not believe in fasts, sacred thread (of Hinduism), or traditional death rites.

The Khalsa must wear the five Ks but must not offend members of other religions.

The Khalsa pray to God before starting work. This is in addition to normal prayers.

Sikhs may learn other languages, but they must learn Punjabi.

Every male must add "Singh" to his name and every female must add "Kaur."

Sikhs must not remove hair from any part of their bodies.

Drugs, smoking, and alcohol are forbidden.

Khalsa men and women must not have their ears or nose pierced.

Sikh women must not wear a face veil.

Sikhs must live on honest labor and give to the poor.

Sikhs must not steal or gamble.

Marriage

In this section you will:

- learn about the Sikh marriage ceremony;
- learn the Sikh teachings about the importance of marriage;
- read and reflect upon some of the Sikh marriage customs.

Marriage is a very important part of Sikhism. Although some marriages are still arranged by the families of the bride and groom, the couple both have the right to reject the partner chosen for them. A marriage brings two families together and **Sikhs** believe it is important that the families can get on with each other. This is why Sikhs do not encourage people to marry outside of their religion.

There is sometimes an engagement ceremony in the **gurdwara,** where God is thanked for bringing the couple together. After this, the groom's mother visits the bride and gives her a gold ring to wear.

Anand karaj—the wedding ceremony

A Sikh wedding usually takes place in the morning and must be held in front of a copy of the **Guru Granth Sahib Ji.** In India, a bride may be dressed very traditionally in red, but elsewhere the bride may wear white and be dressed very simply. Her head will be covered with a chunni (scarf). The groom wears a colored **turban** and scarf, and carries a **kirpan.** Before the service begins there is a ceremony called the **Milna.** The two families meet and give gifts, then eat a meal.

A Sikh wedding in India

Walking around the Guru Granth Sahib Ji

At the marriage, the bride sits on the groom's left, facing the Guru Granth Sahib Ji. The person conducting the service asks the man and woman to stand. The ceremony begins with the morning hymn, **Asa di var,** and **Ardas.**

Any Sikh may conduct a marriage. The first part of the ceremony is an explanation of the Sikh ideal of marriage and the fact that marriage is not just a social contract but the joining together of two souls to become "a single soul in two bodies."

The bride and groom both bow to the Guru Granth Sahib Ji, which shows that they accept these teachings and that they want to spend the rest of their lives together, supporting each other physically and spiritually.

The bride's father places flower garlands over the couple, then takes one end of the groom's scarf and ties it to the end of the bride's head scarf to show that she is leaving her father and joining her husband.

The **Lavan** (wedding hymn) of **Guru** Ram Das Ji is sung and after each of the four verses the couple walk clockwise around the Guru Granth Sahib Ji, the bride following the groom. Each time around, they bow to the Guru Granth Sahib Ji to show that they accept the teachings of the Lavan, which explains the relationship between God and an individual. The couple are reminded to follow this ideal throughout their married life.

The service ends with the sharing of **karah parshad.**

Everyone eats a simple meal in the **langar** after the ceremony, and the bride and groom go to their new home together.

Marriage customs

Sikhs must not choose their marriage partner on the basis of **caste.**

A Sikh's daughter must be married to a Sikh.

A Sikh's marriage should be conducted according to Sikh marriage rites.

Members of other religions cannot be married at the **Anand karaj** ceremony.

Child marriage is forbidden.

No Sikh can accept a marriage partner for their son or daughter on the basis of money.

Sikhs must not consult horoscopes in order to choose the wedding date.

None of the practices of Hindu marriage ceremonies are allowed.

If a Sikh's marriage partner dies, they may remarry if they wish.

Although the guests may give money to the couple, the idea of a dowry is forbidden in Sikhism.

Sikhs are expected to remain faithful to their husband or wife. Sikhs accept that divorce, although unwelcome, is sometimes inevitable.

Widows and widowers are allowed to remarry in a gurdwara.

Death

In this section you will:

- learn about the Sikh funeral ceremonies and the customs Sikhs follow;
- learn about the Sikh teachings about death.

For **Sikhs,** death is not the end. They believe in eternal life in the form of **reincarnation.** This means that a soul may be reborn many times as a human or an animal.

The **Guru Granth Sahib Ji** teaches that the body is simply clothing for the soul and so can be discarded, just as we might throw away old clothes.

Usually, Sikhs cremate their dead. In India this often happens on the day someone dies, but elsewhere it may take place two or three days later, so that people have the chance to travel to the funeral.

When someone is near to death, friends and relatives will come to the bedside and say **Sukhmani** (the Hymn of Peace). The dying person will try to reply **Waheguru** (Wonderful Lord).

A Sikh funeral ceremony. The body is placed in front of the Guru Granth Sahib Ji.

The body is taken for cremation.

The body is washed and dressed in traditional Sikh clothing, including the five Ks—**panj kakke.** Then it is placed in a coffin, taken to the **gurdwara,** and placed in front of the Guru Granth Sahib Ji.

The coffin is carried to the cremation ground in a procession while hymns are sung. In India, it is placed on a funeral pyre, which is then lit by a close relative. As the coffin burns, someone says the evening prayer, the **Kirtan Sohila:**

God has determined the time for my nuptials;
come pour the oil of joy at my door.

Bless me, my friends, that I find that sweet union,
dwelling as one with my Master and Lord.

All must receive their last call from the Master;
daily he summons those souls who must go.

Hold in remembrance the Lord who will
summon you; soon you will hear his command.

Kirtan Sohila

These verses remind Sikhs of their belief that death is just a short sleep before rebirth, and that everyone must remember God in the hope of escaping rebirth and reaching **mukti.**

The relatives and friends of the dead person now return to the gurdwara, where the **Anand Sahib** is sung and **Ardas** is said. The ceremony ends with **karah parshad.**

Mourning

During the next ten days, many families read all of the Guru Granth Sahib Ji. They stay at home and are visited by friends and relatives. Karah parshad and **langar** are prepared by the family and offered to all visitors. Some families arrange an **Akhand Path** (complete reading), or a Sadharan Path (noncontinuous reading), of the Guru Granth Sahib Ji in the gurdwara after a funeral.

Funeral customs

Guru Nanak Dev Ji wanted his followers to show, in all aspects of their lives, that they were no longer Hindus or Muslims, and so he taught that funerals should not be carried out with any of the ceremonials associated with these religions. He also emphasized that the body of the dead person should be shown respect, but was no longer of any value. The important part of the person, the soul, had already left the body to be reborn.

The Sikh belief in reincarnation is very similar to that of Hindus, but Guru Nanak Dev Ji taught that there will be a Last Judgment and that, after this, souls that have been reincarnated will eventually rejoin Waheguru.

Sikh cremations can take place at any time. Sikhs are cremated wearing the **five Ks.** Mourners must not cry out at a funeral or make any public displays of their grief. Hymns are sung until the body is on the funeral pyre, and then a final prayer is said before the pyre is lit.

When the funeral pyre is burned out, all the ashes are gathered up and either poured into running water or buried at the cremation site. Sikhs may not raise tombstones or monuments to the dead.

Creation

In this section you will:

- learn about what Sikhs believe about the creation;
- learn the importance of these beliefs;
- read some Sikh passages about God as creator.

Humans, trees, holy places
Coasts, clouds, fields
Islands, continents, universes
Spheres and solar systems
Life forms—egg-born, womb-born, earth-born, sweat-born
Only God knows their existence
in oceans, mountains, everywhere
Nanak says God created them
and God takes care of them all.

Guru Granth Sahib Ji

Sikhism is based on the "Oneness of Creation." **Sikhs** believe that the universe was made by God who created the earth and all forms of life on it. God is in charge, and arranges the birth, life, and death of everything.

God is responsible for all of creation, Sikhs believe, and everything in and on the earth belongs to God. Without God's **Hukam** (will) nothing can exist, change, or develop.

Sikhs believe that before the creation there was no earth, no sky, no sun, and no life. Only God existed alone until God's decision to create the world. Then God created everything by a single word.

Since creating the world God has cared for it; God looks after it and protects it. There is no single aspect of the earth that God does not care for and so, according to **Guru** Arjan Dev Ji:

Even creatures in rocks and stones are well provided for. Birds who fly thousands of miles away leaving their young ones behind know that they will be sustained and taught to fend for themselves by God.

Sikhs believe that all creatures lead their lives under God's rule.

If I were a doe living in the forest, eating grass and leaves, with God's Grace I will find God. If I were a cuckoo living in the mango tree, contemplating and singing, God reveals through God's mercy.

Guru Granth Sahib Ji

Sikhism teaches that God created five elements—air, water, earth, fire, and space. Everything in nature and the environment is made from these elements. Water is the most important of the elements, but all the elements must be kept in balance to avoid disaster.

God created night and day, seasons, time, and occasions. So also air, water, fire, and nether regions. Amidst these has God fixed the earth, the place for Righteous Activities.

Guru Granth Sahib Ji

Waheguru, the Creator God

Sikhism teaches that it is God, **Waheguru,** who created everything and is in charge of all life, arranging birth, life, and death. God is actively involved in the world, caring for and protecting it and all life under God's will.

There are several passages about God as Creator in the Guru Granth Sahib Ji. Two of these are:

You are the Creator, O Lord, the Unknowable. You created the Universe of diverse kinds, colors, and qualities.

Guru Nanak Dev Ji

The Formless Supreme Being abides in the Realm of Eternity. Over His creation He casts His glance of grace….Of creation worlds upon worlds abide therein; all obedient to His will; he watches over them in bliss, and has each constantly in mind.

Guru Nanak Dev Ji

Environment

In this section you will:

- learn Sikh teachings about caring for the environment;
- learn why these are important for Sikhs;
- read about Sikh attitudes toward people and nature.

Sikhs believe that God created the world as a place where every type of plant and animal could live so that all life could have the chance to prove that it was good enough to reach **mukti.**

Guru Nanak Dev Ji taught that:

Nature we see
Nature we hear
Nature we observe with awe, wonder, and joy
Nature in the nether regions
Nature in the skies
Nature in the whole creation

Nature in the sacred texts (Vedas, Puranas, and Qur'an)
Nature in all reflection
Nature in food, in water, in garments, and in love for all
Nature in species, kinds, colors
Nature in life forms
Nature in good deeds
Nature in pride and in ego
Nature in air, water, and fire
Nature in the soil of the earth
All nature is yours, O powerful Creator
You command it, observe it, and pervade within it

Guru Granth Sahib Ji

Although Sikhs believe that humans are the stewards of the earth and have to look after it, they also believe that God's spirit is in everything. Therefore many Sikhs are vegetarians.

Believing that causing damage to the environment is harmful, Sikhs try to take care not to disturb the balance of nature.

This Sikh man plants trees to do his part in helping the environment.

authority always;
Earn an honest living—do not take what does not belong to you, or more than you need—essential truths for a proper relationship with nature;
Share with others—this includes all creation, not just human beings.

Guru Granth Sahib Ji

Oil pollution damages the environment.

In the Punjab, rainfall is vital and always welcomed. When the monsoon arrives Sikhs celebrate because God has been good to them.

The lives of the **Gurus** are full of stories of their love for nature. Therefore, Sikhs are forbidden to kill for the sake of killing or in order to eat to excess.

In Sikh hymns, God is praised as the provider of all life. There is no difference between the world of humans and the world of nature. Both are equally important and must be treated with respect.

The Gurus have strongly made us aware of our responsibility toward this earth.

Guru Granth Sahib Ji

Sikhs believe that the environment can only be preserved if the balance that God created is maintained. The principles for this are found in the Guru Granth Sahib Ji.

Pray to God—remember God and God's

Caring for life

Sikhism was founded in the Punjab in northwest India. The geographical situation of Punjab is such that rainfall is essential and therefore always welcomed. The arrival of rain is an occasion for rejoicing. Water is seen as a source of life. It produces the vegetation that is used as food for humans and fodder for animals.

Sikhism teaches that the natural environment and the survival of all life forms are closely linked in the rythm of nature. It is for this reason that, in Sikhism, those who kill for lust of hunting, eating, or to make sacrifices are condemned. In Sikh hymns, God is often referred to as the provider of all life. God, as both father and mother, guarantees equality to man and woman in faith and compassion toward all beings and nature.

Sikhs believe that humans and nature were created simultaneously from the same light. Therefore, we share the world with nature and with our fellow beings. Sikh Gurus have attempted to warn those who desire to control nature and the world in which we live.

Adapted from *The Sikh Statement on Nature* made at Assisi, Italy, 1986

Human Rights

In this section you will:

- learn Sikh teachings about human rights;
- learn what Sikhism says about equality;
- read about the way in which Sikhs are working towards having an independent homeland.

It is a very important teaching of Sikhism, both in the **Guru Granth Sahib Ji** and in everyday life, that everyone is equal regardless of race, sex, class, **caste,** or religion. Any hungry person who visits a **gurdwara** will always be fed.

A Hindu Brahmin of the priestly caste. Guru Nanak Dev Ji taught that the caste system is wrong.

Sikhs believe that God, who is the creator and source of all forms of life, is without any form, sex, or color. Therefore, any differences that are visible between humans whom God created are irrelevant—they do not make any one person better than any other. Any act of kindness that is performed toward another human being is an act of respect toward creation and is seen as an act of worship of God.

Guru Nanak Dev Ji was born a Hindu, and Sikhism has kept some of the teachings of Hinduism. For example, Hinduism also welcomes people of all religious beliefs. However, Guru Nanak Dev Ji taught that the caste system of Hinduism was wrong.

There are four varnas (castes), which form divisions within Hindu society. Within these varnas, there are also many jati (caste groups). Hindus believe that every Hindu is born into a particular caste because of past behavior in a previous life, and that these castes cannot be changed. The first and highest caste is the Brahmin (teacher or priest), the second is the Kshatriya (ruler or warrior), the third is the Vaishya (merchant or farmer) and the fourth is the Shudra (servant or laborer).

People who are born below any of these castes are thought of as untouchables or outcasts, and are sometimes called dalit (oppressed). The caste system affects almost everything a Hindu does. Marriages should only take place between members of the same caste. Some Hindus will not eat with, or take food from, members of castes lower than theirs.

When Guru Nanak Dev Ji founded Sikhism, he intended that the discrimination of the caste system would be abolished. Unfortunately, some people still believe that it is important and it can sometimes influence aspects of Sikh life such as marriage, where members of one group may be unwilling to marry a member of another. However, Sikhs are taught to treat all people equally and hope to be treated the same.

The langar is a place where Sikhs can offer hospitality to all.

A Sikh independent homeland

One of the major problems for Sikhs today in seeking equality is Khalistan. In 1799, Maharaja Ranjit Singh established Lahore as the capital of an independent Sikh state where true equality among Sikhs, Muslims, Hindus, and others was practiced. After his death in 1839, there were problems with the next two leaders and two wars were fought. The British took over the Punjab in 1849 and ended Sikh independence.

When India became independent from Britain in 1947, two countries were established: India was mainly Hindu and Pakistan was mainly Muslim. The Sikh homeland of the Punjab was split between India and Pakistan. Sikhs asked for independence, but it was not given to them.

In 1966, the Indian government agreed that the province of the Punjab should have Punjabi as its official language and that Sikhs should represent the province in the Punjabi Suba (assembly). However, Sikhs are still working to reunite the Punjab into one country of their own.

The Punjab

In 1709–1710, a Sikh leader, Bandha Singh Bahadur, freed the Punjab from Mogul rule. The Sikhs built the land into a powerful kingdom under Ranjit Singh (1780–1839).

In 1849, the Punjab came under British rule, when the British took over India. In 1947, when India gained its independence from Britain, the Punjab was split between Hindu-governed India and Muslim-ruled Pakistan.

In 1966, the Punjab was divided in two. The new, smaller state of Punjab has its capital at Chandigarh.

By 1980, many Sikhs were campaigning for a totally independent Sikh homeland: Khalistan—Land of the Pure. Since then, there have been several episodes of fighting between some Sikh militants and the Indian authorities, and the question of a Sikh homeland has still not been solved.

Service to Others 1—Sewa

In this section you will:

● learn about sewa;

● learn why this idea is so important to Sikhs;

● read about how this teaching might affect people.

It is very important for all **Sikhs** to provide a service to the community. This is called **sewa,** and includes service to the Sikh community itself and to others. Sikhs believe in being prepared to give up some of their time and energy to help others. Sikhism comprises service to God, to the **Khalsa,** and to all of humanity.

Tan, or physical service: helping in the langar

Sikhism teaches that a person should try to become less self-centered (**manmukh**) and more God-centered (**gurmukh**), and so live their lives in the selfless service of others (sewa).

Although **Nam Simran,** remembering God, is central to Sikhism, this must be combined with sewa. The following from the **Guru Granth Sahib Ji** emphasizes this point:

True worship consists in the meditation of God's name… There can be no worship without performing good deeds.

Guru Granth Sahib Ji

There are three different aspects of sewa.

● **Tan:** This is physical service, and might include working in the **langar** and helping to look after the **gurdwara.** Providing langar for the congregation is seen as a privilege as well as a duty.

● **Man:** This is mental service. Sikhs might do this by studying the Guru Granth Sahib Ji and teaching it to others.

● **Dhan:** This is material service to other people. Sikhs might give money to charities or give their time to help people who are in need. It might also include building a school or a hospital, visiting the sick, or caring for disaster victims.

None of these services should be performed for personal gain, but because a Sikh wants to serve God. Therefore, in all of these ways, Sikhs can perform sewa and so serve God and the world.

The **Gurus** themselves set the example of sewa by often performing basic tasks that some people would have considered to be beneath them, for example, cleaning the gurdwara.

Tan, or physical service: sweeping the pavements of the Golden Temple

A place in God's court can only be attained if we do service to others in this world… Wandering ascetics, warriors, celibates, holy men, none of them can obtain **mukti** without performing sewa.

Guru Granth Sahib Ji

Serving others

The Sikh **Gurus** said that sewa, the performance of selfless service to others, was the first step toward being a Sikh. A person who does service without payment or any hope of a reward is called a Sewak or Sewadar. Performing sewa makes people humble and, in this way, the name of God can enter into their minds.

A Sewak must follow the code of self-discipline given by the Gurus. Sewa, or voluntary service, can be done with the body or the mind, or with money.

Example of sewa

Physical service might be cleaning or looking after shoes at the gurdwara, or cooking in the langar. Sikhs might help the community or their family with cash or with labor They might also give money to poor people and charities. Service with the mind may be thinking about the **Gurbani,** and remembering and repeating God's name. Anyone who performs sewa with the idea of gaining from it is not acting as a true Sikh. In India, Sikhs run orphanages, homes for widows, and hospitals, schools, and institutes for the poor and disabled.

Service to Others 2

In this section you will:

● learn about Sikh principles of life;

● learn why these ideas are important to Sikhs;

● read about five values that are important to Sikhs.

The **Gurus** said that **Sikhs** should live their lives according to three principles, which are all equally important.

● **Nam Simran:** to remember the name of God. This can be done by meditating on God's name.

● **Kirat karna:** to earn a living by honest means.

● **Vand chhakna:** to share everything in charity with people who are less fortunate. This includes time, abilities, and money.

These teachings were designed so that Sikhs would not think of the religious side of their lives as being separate from the rest of their lives. Prayer, hard work, and generosity are all equally important in living a good life. Sikhs are discouraged from spending all their time on the religious aspects of life, for example, prayer. They must live lives that are complete and that contribute to the welfare of the community.

Kirat karna

Kirat karna means that Sikhs must earn their living honestly. Work is essential for the individual, the family, and the community, and a Sikh has a duty to provide for basic needs. Everyone has a responsibility to earn a living if he or she possibly can. It does not matter what the work is, whether it is professional skills or manual labor, provided that it is honest and not against the teachings of the Gurus. So, a Sikh should never earn money from selling illegal drugs or doing something that might take advantage of other people.

Sikhism teaches that it is not wrong to be rich provided the money is gained honestly, but that it is wrong to live your life just in order to make a lot of money. The money a Sikh earns is used for his or her family, and also for the **Khalsa** and the community as a whole.

A Sikh hospital in Nairobi

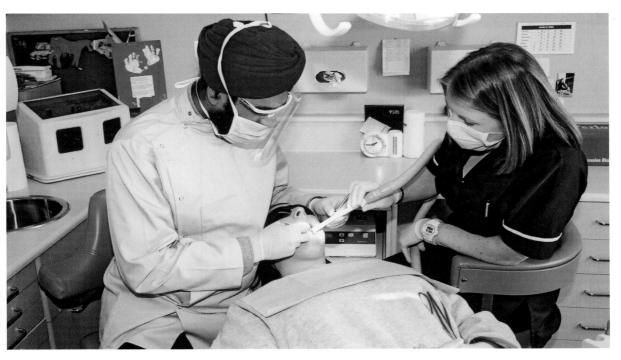

A Sikh dentist can help others through his work.

Vand chhakna

Vand chhakna teaches Sikhs that they should live their lives on the principles of generosity and self-sacrifice.

Guru Amar Das Ji taught Sikhs the principle of **daswandh.** This means giving a tenth of surplus money to the community. Money given in this way may be used for building schools or hospitals, or to help those who are poor or suffering. It is up to individuals to decide how much they should give.

Three virtues

The first virtue for Sikhs is truth. According to Guru Nanak Dev Ji, "Truth is the remedy for all ills, it washes away all sins." "Truthful living" is a life lived according to the example of the Sikh Gurus.

The second virtue is contentment. Someone who is contented is free from ambition, envy, greed, and jealousy.

Patience gives people courage to put up with all the problems of everyday life.

Faith and compassion

The fourth virtue for Sikhs is perfect faith in the Gurus. Although Sikhs may feel that they are being tested, they must never lose faith or follow anyone except the Gurus.

The fifth virtue is compassion. This means looking at someone else's problem as your own, and doing everything you can to relieve it. It also means overlooking failings in other people.

Women in Sikhism

In this section you will:

- learn about the Sikh attitude toward women;
- understand why this is an important part of Sikh life and teaching;
- read about the role of women in the gurdwara.

Sikhism is one of the few religions where women have an equal role with men within the faith. Within the **Sikh** community, a woman can choose her own way of life, and many Sikh women are now continuing their education through college in order to fulfill their ambition for a professional career.

When there is any suggestion that Sikhism is treating women differently from men, this is because of society and history and it goes against the teachings of the **Gurus.** Women can be members of the **Khalsa,** undergoing exactly the same ceremony as men, and can become **granthi**—leading the worship in the **gurdwara.**

We are God's own people, neither high nor low nor in between… Religion consists not in mere talk. He who looks on all alike and considers all to be equal is acclaimed as truly religious.

Guru Granth Sahib Ji

Guru Nanak Dev Ji taught that:

From women born, shaped in the womb, to woman betrothed and wed;
We are bound to women by ties of affection, on women man's future depends.
If one woman dies he seeks another; with a woman he orders his life.
Why then should one speak evil of women, they who give birth to kings?
Women also are born from women; none takes birth except from a woman.
Only the True One, Nanak, needs no help from a woman.
Blessed are they, both men and women, who endlessly praise their Lord.
Blessed are they in the True One's court; there shall their faces shine.

Guru Granth Sahib Ji

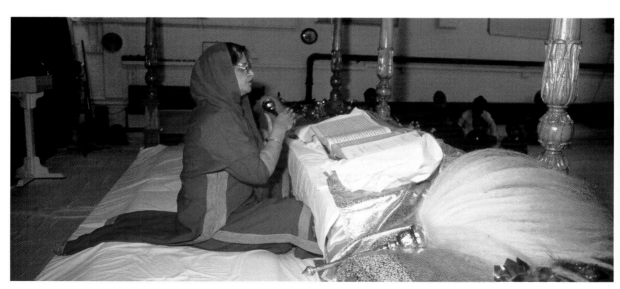

A woman granthi leads the worship in the gurdwara.

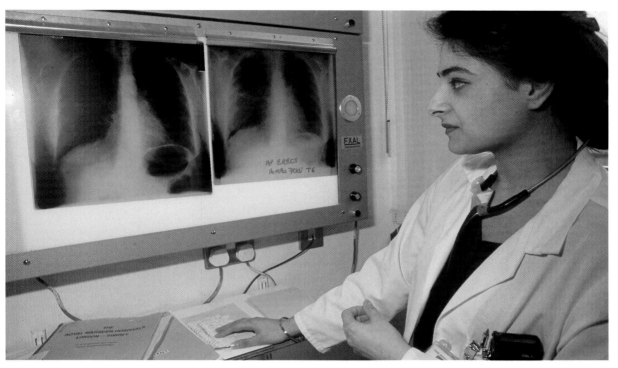

Sikh women are able to work in any field, for example, medicine.

The Gurus also condemned some Hindu practices, including giving dowries to a man to marry a particular woman, and suttee, the idea that when a man dies his wife should kill herself on his funeral pyre.

In the gurdwara

Men and women sit separately in the gurdwara. This is done so that no one touches the wife or husband of another person by accident. Sikhism also says that if men and women sit together, they may find it difficult to concentrate on the hymns.

There is no particular side of the gurdwara for men or women to sit. If more women than men are expected then the women sit on the larger side. The custom is that, normally, people sit on the side where they sat on the first day the gurdwara was used.

Women granthis

Both men and women can perform the duties of a granthi in a gurdwara. There is no discrimination against any Sikh being a granthi. There are more male granthis than women because, particularly in a gurdwara where the granthi is a full-time job, a woman with children might find it difficult to carry out the duties. Sometimes, a husband and wife will share the duties of the granthi.

The true equality of men and women is a very important aspect of Sikh life and teaching. Where there does appear to be any discrimination, this is cultural and not in the teachings of the Gurus.

Glossary

Adi Granth collection of the hymns of the first four Gurus and some of those of Guru Arjan Dev Ji

Akal Takht "Throne of the Eternal." The building facing the Golden Temple in Amritsar

Akhand Path continuous reading of the Guru Granth Sahib Ji from beginning to end

Amrit "nectar." Sanctified liquid made of sugar and water, used in initiation ceremonies

Amritsar city in the Punjab and the location of the Golden Temple

Amritvela early morning prayer and meditation

Anand karaj "Ceremony of bliss." The wedding ceremony

Anand Sahib "Hymn of bliss"

Anandpur Sahib town in a valley at the foot of the Himalayas. The ashes of the head of Guru Tegh Bahadur Ji are buried there. It is also the place where Guru Gobind Singh Ji founded the Khalsa.

Ardas prayer offered during most religious acts

Asa di var the morning hymn

Baisakhi major Sikh festival celebrating the formation of the Khalsa in 1699

Bhakti devotion to God, worship

Caste different levels of social groups that Hindus believe people are born into

Chanani canopy over the scriptures, used as a mark of respect

Chauri symbol of the authority of the Guru Granth Sahib Ji. A fan waved over scriptures, made of yak hairs or nylon.

Dasam Granth collection of compositions, some of which are attributed to the tenth Sikh Guru, Guru Gobind Singh Ji, compiled some years after his death

Daswandh giving a tenth of surplus money to the community

Dhan material service to other people

Divali Mela festival that marks the end of the rainy season and the escape and return to Amritsar of Guru Har Gobind Ji

Diwan congregational worship

Five Ks *see* **Panj kakke**

Goindwal location of a deep well, or baoli, built by Guru Amar Das Ji

Golak long box in which worshipers place their offering of money

Granthi reader of the Guru Granth Sahib Ji, who officiates at ceremonies

Gurbani word of God revealed by the Gurus; also the Shabads, contained in the Guru Granth Sahib Ji

Gurdwara Sikh place of worship. Literally the "doorway to the Guru"

Gurmukh someone who lives by the Guru's teaching

Gurmukhi "from the Guru's mouth." The name given to the script in which the scriptures and the Punjabi language are written.

Gurpurbs Guru's anniversary (birth or death). This term is also used for other anniversaries, for example, the installation of the Adi Granth in 1604.

Guru teacher. In Sikhism, the title of Guru is used for the ten human Gurus and the Guru Granth Sahib Ji

Guru Granth Sahib Ji Sikh scriptures, compiled by Guru Arjan Dev Ji and given its final form by Guru Gobind Singh Ji

Guru Nanak Dev Ji (1469–1539) first Guru and the founder of the Sikh faith

Gutka collection of hymns

Harimandir Sahib Golden Temple in Amritsar

Hola Mohalla Mela festival that celebrates Guru Gobind Singh Ji holding a three-day festival at Anandpur

Hukam "God's will"

Ik Onkar "There is only One God." The first phrase of the Mool Mantar. It is also used as a symbol to decorate Sikh objects

Japji Sahib morning prayer, composed by Guru Nanak Dev Ji, which forms the first chapter of the Guru Granth Sahib Ji

Kachera traditional shorts or underwear. One of the five Ks

Kangha comb worn in the hair. One of the five Ks

Kara steel or iron band worn on the right wrist. One of the five Ks

Karah parshad sanctified food distributed at Sikh ceremonies

Karma actions and their consequences

Kaur "Princess." Name given to all Sikh females

Kesh uncut hair. One of the five Ks

Khalsa "Community of the pure." The Sikh community

Khanda double-edged sword used in the initiation ceremony. Also used as the emblem on the Sikh flag

Kirat karna earning one's livelihood by one's own efforts

Kirpan sword. One of the five Ks

Kirtan devotional singing of the compositions found in the Guru Granth Sahib Ji

Kirtan Sohila prayer said before going to sleep. It is also used at the cremation ceremony and when the Guru Granth Sahib Ji is laid to rest.

Langar "Guru's kitchen." The gurdwara dining hall and the food served in it

Lavan four verses that are sung at a wedding ceremony

Mala prayer beads

Manji sahib small platform on which the scripture is placed

Manmukh thinking about oneself first

Mela "fair." Describes Sikh festivals that are not gurpurbs

Milna ceremony that takes place before the wedding service

Mool Mantar "basic teaching." The statement of beliefs at the beginning of the Guru Granth Sahib Ji

Mukti escape from rebirth

Nam Japna remembering the name of God

Nam Simran meditation on the divine name, using passages of scripture

Nishan Sahib the Sikh flag, flown at gurdwaras

Nit nem saying the specified daily prayers

Pakha fan used by Sikhs walking with the Gurus, keeping them cool in the hot areas of the Punjab

Palanquin special carriage

Panj kakke "the five Ks." The symbols of Sikhism worn by Sikhs

Panj piare "the five beloved ones." Those first initiated into the Khalsa; those who perform the rite today

Ragi Sikh musician who sings compositions from the Guru Granth Sahib Ji

Reincarnation belief that people are reborn after death

Romalla cloth on which the Guru Granth Sahib Ji is placed

Sadhsangat congregation or assembly of Sikhs

Sahaj-dhari "seekers after God." Sikhs who are not members of the Khalsa

Serovar pool around the Golden Temple in Amritsar

Sewa selfless service directed at the sadhsangat and gurdwara, and also to humanity in general

Shabads hymns from the Guru Granth Sahib Ji, the divine word

Sikh "learner"; "disciple." Person who believes in the ten Gurus and the Guru Granth Sahib Ji, and who has no other religion

Singh "Lion." Name adopted by all Sikh males

Sodar Rahiras prayer said before the evening meal

Sukhmani the Hymn of Peace

Tan physical service

Turban head covering worn by many Sikhs

Vand chhakna sharing one's time, talents, and earnings with the less fortunate

Waheguru "Wonderful Lord." A Sikh name for God

Yatras visits to places associated with the Gurus and Sikhism

Index